THINK YOU KNOW IT ALL?

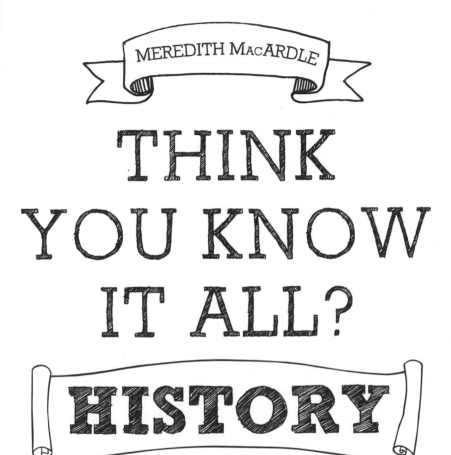

THINK YOU KNOW IT ALL?

THE ACTIVITY BOOK FOR GROWN-UPS

Michael O'Mara Books Limited

First published in Great Britain in 2020 by
Michael O'Mara Books Limited
9 Lion Yard
Tremadoc Road
London SW4 7NQ

A CIP catalogue record for this book is available from the British Library.

Papers used by Michael O'Mara Books Limited are natural, recyclable products made from wood grown in sustainable forests. The manufacturing processes conform to the environmental regulations of the country of origin.

ISBN: 978-1-78929-232-9

1 2 3 4 5 6 7 8 9 10

www.mombooks.com

Illustrations by David Woodroffe, Meredith MacArdle
and Barbara Ward
Additional picture credits: page 25 ZU_09 / iStock;
page 62 Everett Historical / Shutterstock; page 105 Shutterstock

Cover design by Ana Bjezancevic
Designed and typeset by Allan Somerville

Printed in the UK by CPI Group (UK) Ltd,
Croydon, CR0 4YY

DEDICATION

For Lucas

INTRODUCTION

History buffs literally have the whole world and the whole human story to enjoy and learn about. And that's exactly what this book is going to test you on.

Questions run from prehistory up to the huge global changes that were seen after the Second World War. Important events and significant people from any period of history and any country are covered, so there will be something to challenge everyone, whatever your depth of knowledge or area of interest.

Perhaps you think you know it all about the history of art and architecture, the development of science, or military history, or exploration, or films? Do you fancy yourself a medievalist or a bit of a Napoleonic expert? Then take the challenge and prove that you know it all.

This is not an ordinary quiz book. It offers plenty of questions that demand a straightforward right or wrong answer but there are also activities to complete. You will find yourself needing to trace a maze, decipher a pictogram, spot the difference in a picture, identify a map, or fill in a crossword in Latin. (Don't worry, if you've not heard of any Roman emperors at all, you'll still be able to have a go.)

History might be linear and flow one way but this book adds to the fun by not following any chronological order or subject structure. You'll need to turn your mind from famous rulers to great art, from wars to medical discoveries. There's something at all levels and on all topics. So, you can't rest on your laurels, even if you think you do know it all about your special interests.

If you can't complete a question, don't give up and turn to the solution at once. Take your time and come back to the question. You never know what extra knowledge you might be able to bring up from the depths of your memory. Or take a good guess or use the process of elimination. Even if you do have to resort to looking up an answer, at least you will have the satisfaction of learning more about our wonderful history.

And if you can answer a question then congratulations. You do know all about that one but what about the next question? And the one after that? And after that?

With space on the pages for you to puzzle out your answers, all you need is a pen or a pencil to get going, so let's see if you do know it all about what happened in the past ...

SO...THINK YOU KNOW IT ALL ABOUT HISTORY?

Nicknames

What were the nicknames of these historical figures?

A. King Richard I of England

B. Isabella of France

C. General Erwin Rommel

D. Otto von Bismarck

E. Louis XIV of France

F. Simón Bolívar

G. Rosie, a symbol of working women in the USA during the Second World War

Engineless

Which one of these people was not involved in the development of internal combustion engines and cars?

Clément Ader
Karl Benz
Gottlieb Daimler
Nicolaus Otto

Answers on page 166

Laughing at the Past

Name the historical settings that feature in these humorous films:

1. Buster Keaton's *The General*

2. Charlie Chaplin's *The Great Dictator*

3. Mel Brooks' *Blazing Saddles*

4. In the film *Les Visiteurs*, what period of history do the hapless French time travellers come from?

5. The British *Carry On* series produced a film poking fun at British colonialism called *Carry On Up the –*?

Answers on page 166

Dynastic Duo

Through a series of dynastic marriages, which fifteenth- to sixteenth-century Spanish couple were the ancestors of every European monarch who sat on a throne in 2020?

Worthless

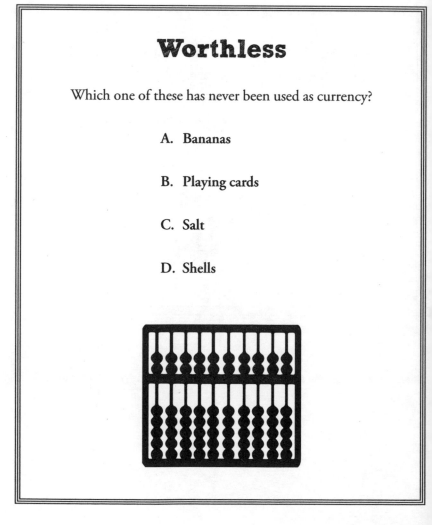

Which one of these has never been used as currency?

A. Bananas

B. Playing cards

C. Salt

D. Shells

Answers on pages166

Hidden Treasures

How many objects can you find in this ancient Egyptian tomb? One of the items does not belong. Which one is it?

Answers on page 166

Food Facts and Fables

Are these statements about food history true or false?

1. The Indian dish kedgeree was invented by British cooks during the days of the British Raj in India.

2. Dry food mixes were first produced during the Industrial Revolution in Britain.

3. Hamburgers are so named because they were first made of ham rather than any other meat.

4. In America, pizzas were only known in a few east-coast cities until servicemen returned from Italy after the First World War and created a countrywide demand.

5. According to a contemporary travel book, the sandwich was named after John Montagu, the 4th Earl of Sandwich in England. It is said that in 1762 he called for food that he could hold and eat in one hand so he could carry on playing at cards, and was given salt beef sandwiched between slices of toasted bread.

6. Chinese fortune cookies were first made in 1911 to celebrate the Chinese revolution.

7. Chicken Marengo is said to be named after a battle in 1800 during which Napoleon Bonaparte's French armies defeated the Austrians. While commanding the battle, Napoleon demanded a meal at once, so the dish was cobbled together from whatever ingredients his steward could find.

8. Some of the early tin cans in the nineteenth century were made with a lead alloy seal, which could result in poisoning if the lead contaminated the tin's food contents.

9. Cocaine, one of the original ingredients of Coca-Cola, was taken out of the drink in 1943.

10. In her popular book *Mrs Beeton's Book of Household Management* (1861), the Victorian British writer Isabella Beeton invented the recipe for paella.

Island Ban

Which traditional Hawaiian practice, frequently performed nowadays, was temporarily banned as a 'pagan' practice in 1830?

Answers on pages 166-7

Important Elevens

What was the significance of 11/11/11 in 1918?

Answer on page 167

Roman Mini Crossword

Answer the clues with the LATIN word. The letters in the grey boxes can be rearranged to form an important Roman road.

ACROSS

4. Situated in Apulia, southern Italy, one of Rome's few disastrous defeats, inflicted by Hannibal of Carthage.
5. First name, in Latin, of a Roman general, lover of Cleopatra, immortalized in a play by William Shakespeare.
6. Brother of Romulus, legendary founders of Rome.
7. Most common first name of a famous general who was assassinated in the Forum.

DOWN

1. First name of the wife of Emperor Augustus.
2. Roman goddess of love, the equivalent of the Greek goddess Aphrodite.
3. Roman city covered with volcanic ash and pumice in AD 79.
4. Family name of a politician, philosopher, writer and orator, who wrote *De re publica* and also wrote 'A room without books is like a body without a soul.'

1
2
3
4
5
6

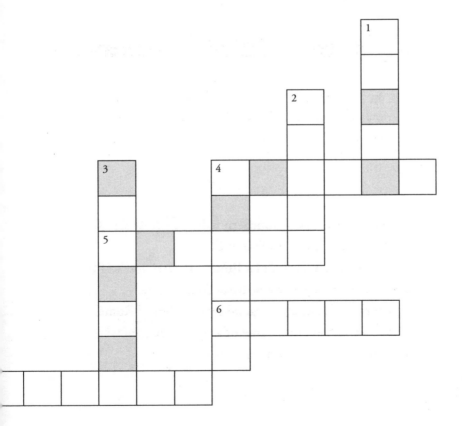

Answers on page 168

Film Night, Part 1

1. Which earthly polities fought the real 'star wars' series of conflicts?

2. The Hollywood western *The Magnificent Seven* was based on which Japanese film featuring historic warriors?

3. In *Rabbit-Proof Fence*, what policy, common in many colonized countries, was implemented against aboriginal Australian children?

4. What battle is fought in *Zulu*?

5. What city burns during *Gone With the Wind*, and was it in the Northern or Southern states during the American Civil War?

6. In the film *Lawrence of Arabia*, Alec Guinness plays Prince Faisal. After the First World War ended, what positions did Faisal hold?

Answers on page 168

A Romantic Sport?

Jane Austen's novel *Northanger Abbey*, completed in 1803, contains the first literary mention of which sport?

A. Polo
B. Baseball
C. Rugby

Answer on page 169

The Tale of Troy

Fill in the gaps in this story:

The most poetic account of the Trojan War is the *Iliad*, by the Greek poet ____ . It is called 'Iliad' because the Greek name for Troy was ____ . We also know the story from several other pieces of ancient Greek writings, such as the play *The Trojan Women*, by ____ . The central woman in the story, Helen, is known as Helen of Troy, although she was a Greek and was married to the Mycenean king ____ . The war began because she ran off with ____ , a prince of ____ . The Greeks besieged Troy to get Helen back, and ____ years of warfare ensued. Eventually the city fell to a trick, when the Greeks built what is known as the Trojan ____ . One of the Greek warriors was Achilles, who was the great hero of a later Macedonian warlord, called ____ . While marching to conquer 'the known world', this Macedonian made a detour to visit the grave of Achilles. The Trojan War was thought to be a myth until the German archaeologist Heinrich ____ discovered the city in the 1870s. Troy was in fact a wealthy trade city in Asia Minor in the modern country of ____ . Schliemann went on to discover graves of Greek leaders contemporaneous with Troy. In one of them he found a golden death mask known as the Mask of ____ , the overall Greek commander during the Trojan War.

Answers on page 169

Footsteps Pictogram

Which twentieth-century event does this represent?

Answer on page 169

A Common Touch, Part 1

What did the following women have in common?

Mary, Queen of Scots

Queen Elizabeth I of England

Elizabeth Siddall, artist, poet and model for the Pre-Raphaelite Brotherhood artists

Answer on page 169

Prehistoric Hairstyles and Hats

1. A partly preserved body discovered in peat in Clonycavan, County Meath, Ireland, dates back to between 392 and 201 BC, during the Iron Age. 'Clonycavan Man' is one of several 'bog bodies' found in northern Europe, but this one is distinguished by his hairstyle and use of cosmetics to prepare it. A similar hairstyle is not uncommon today, and is named after a style worn by men of some Native American peoples. Ironically, the people it is named after actually had a slightly different style. What is it usually called?

2. 'Tollund Man' is another well-preserved body found in peat, this time in Denmark. He died between 375 and 210 BC, and wore a pointy hat similar to many worn today. What was his cap made of?

A) Sheepskin / wool
B) Leather
C) Wolf's hair

3. In 1991 the mummy of an even more ancient man was found preserved by ice in the Alps. Known as Ötzi, the 'Ice Man', he lived between 3400 and 3100 BC.

I) What period of prehistory is this?

II) Ötzi is the oldest known mummy to have certain bodily ornaments. He had sixty-one in all. What were they?

A) Piercings
B) Loose jewellery
C) Tattoos

III) Ötzi also wore a hat. What material was it made of?

A) Wolfskin
B) Bearskin
C) Rabbit fur

4. The hats worn by Tollund Man and Ötzi shared a certain feature. What was that?

5. Finally, archaeologists think that all three of these men had a common fate. What was it?

Answers on page 169

Scientific Time Travel

You have been possessed of pure scientific genius and have built a time machine. Congratulations, you are in line to win a Nobel Prize: in fact, you are undoubtedly in line for as many Nobel Prizes as different years that you visit. However, your time machine is a bit temperamental and will only go back in time once in every round trip. So your first journey will be into the past, then from that point you can only go forward in time until you return home and reset the machine.

You decide to celebrate your achievement by visiting great scientific figures throughout history, or the moments that great discoveries were made. Remember, you have to start at the oldest date and work your way forward in time, so in what order do you go to visit these people, places or events?

A. Alexander Graham Bell making the first telephone call.

B. Isaac Newton pondering gravity and developing his laws of motion and gravity. Did something really hit him on the head? What was that something?

C. Indian mathematician Aryabhata. Which important mathematical concept did he realize, or did he just develop it?

D. Alexander Fleming looking in dismay at a growth of mould, that accidentally led to his discovery of what?

E. Marie Curie being appointed the first female professor at the University of Paris. What scientific term did she coin?

Answers on page 170

Name the Historian

Can you match these early historians to their works?

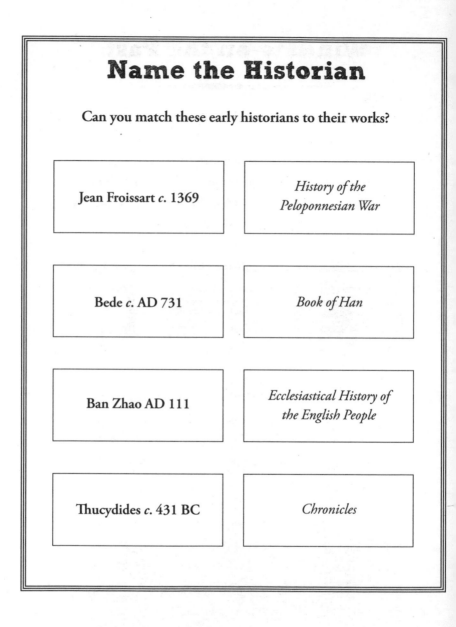

Jean Froissart *c.* 1369	*History of the Peloponnesian War*
Bede *c.* AD 731	*Book of Han*
Ban Zhao AD 111	*Ecclesiastical History of the English People*
Thucydides *c.* 431 BC	*Chronicles*

Answers on page 170

Window on the Past

What event of 1618 in a Central European city is pictured here?

A similar event with the same name, in the same city, took place in 1419. (Some historians give the same name to yet another such occurrence in 1483, although others consider it far less significant.)

Answer on page 170

Peace Treaty

The peace treaty that formally ended the First World War was signed in the Hall of Mirrors in which building that gave its name to the treaty?

Answer on page 170

Colourful Soldiers

Can you identify these colourful soldiers and match them to their nations?

Red Army	UK
Redshirts	Caucasus / Eastern Europe
Redcoats	The Netherlands
Brownshirts	USSR
Blackshirts	Russia
Golden Horde	Italy / UK
William of Orange (William I, Prince of Orange)	Germany
White Guard	Italy

Answers on page 171

First World War Campaign

What was the name of the campaign in the First World War that involved an amphibious assault by the Entente nations on part of modern Turkey?

A Reluctant Road

Between 1830 and 1850 Native American peoples in the Southeastern United States were forcibly moved to west of the Mississippi River.

What was the name of the area they were forced to travel to?

Derived from a description in 1838, what is the collective term for their travels west?

Answers on page 171

Ottoman Glory

The sixteenth-century sultan who expanded the Ottoman Empire and made it a great world power was Suleiman I, the Lawgiver.

He is also often known by what other title?

A Naval Clash

Which important naval and aerial battle of the Second World War took place in the Pacific in early June 1942?

A. Midway
B. Westway
C. Eastway

1. **Who won the battle, and what was its significance?**

2. **How did the defeated government report on the battle to the public, and what happened to the defeated survivors who returned home?**

3. **What happened before the battle that greatly aided the victors?**

Answers on page 172

First World War Maze

Can you help this poor soldier work his way through the Western Front battlefields of the First World War to reach the (dubious) safety of a trench?

Bombs, explosions, barbed wire and muddy pits in his path will all send the soldier back to retrace his steps.

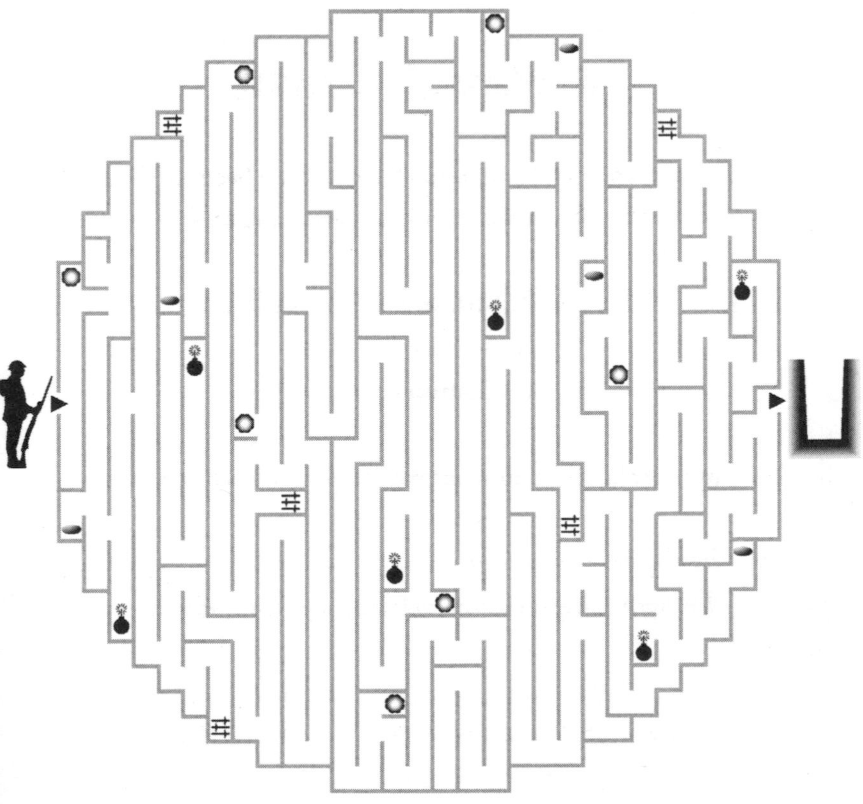

Answers on pages 172-3

Monkey Puzzle

In 1859, a British scientist published a book that was widely mocked by the press of the day, especially in cartoons they published of monkeys wearing clothes and engaging in human activities.

What book inspired this disbelief, who wrote it, and what idea did it promote?

Award yourself a virtual bonus point if you can say the book's full original title.

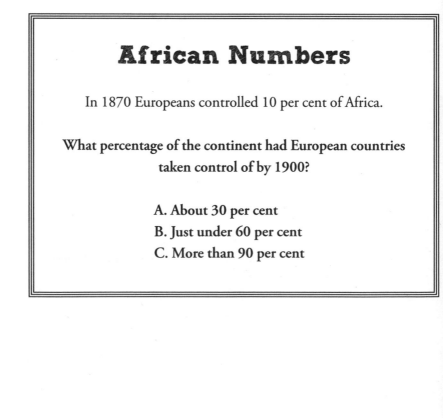

African Numbers

In 1870 Europeans controlled 10 per cent of Africa.

What percentage of the continent had European countries taken control of by 1900?

A. About 30 per cent
B. Just under 60 per cent
C. More than 90 per cent

Answers on page 173

City Nicknames

Match the nickname, and the origin of the nickname, to the city (or part of the city).

City of 100 Spires	Royal palace complex	Rome, Italy
City of Light	The ancients believed the city would last for ever	Amsterdam, the Netherlands
Forbidden City	A large number of canals	Prague, Czech Republic
Eternal City	Originally used to describe the city's horseracing tracks and races	London, UK
Big Apple	Thick smogs due to pollution in the twentieth century	Beijing, China
Venice of the North	Centre of the European Age of Enlightenment	New York City, USA
Big Smoke	A nineteenth-century mathematician counted them	Paris, France

Answers on page 174

Point out the Pyramids

Pyramids were built in many ancient and historic cultures.

Which one of these did not build pyramids?

A. Nubia / Sudan
B. Egypt
C. Merovingian France
D. Meso-America
E. The Chola Empire of India
F. Megalithic cultures in Indonesia

Women Who Made History

Identify these women who made their mark on the past:

1. The Native American woman who helped the English colony at Jamestown, America, in the early seventeenth century

2. The 'Maid of Orleans' who relieved the English siege of Orleans during the Hundred Years War

3. A female Japanese samurai warrior of the early Middle Ages who fought for the Minamoto clan against the Taira clan

4. The seventh-century empress who was the only woman to rule China in her own right

Answers on pages 174

Rebellious Thirteen

When the American Revolution began, there were thirteen British colonies that rebelled against British rule.

Can you name them all?

1.

2.

3.

4.

5.

6.

7.

8.

9.

10.

11.

12.

13.

Answers on page 175

Events of the Second World War

Match these events to their locations:

The Battle of El-Alamein	Hawaii
The Blitz	Amsterdam
The biggest tank battle in history	Monte Cassino, Italy
Pearl Harbor	Kursk, Russia
A protracted battle for control of a monastery strongpoint	Egypt
Anne Frank's refuge	UK

Counting the Stars

Which Meso-American civilization had a particularly complex writing system, an extremely accurate calendar, as well as a precise astronomical system?

Answers on page 175

Travellers' Tales

Who said or wrote these quotes:

1. 'These … are a very good people … they supposed that I was afraid of their bows; and, taking their arrows, they broke them in pieces and threw them into the fire.'

____

2. 'Following the light of the sun, we left the Old World.'

____

3. 'Do the difficult things while they are easy and do the great things while they are small. A journey of a thousand miles must begin with a single step.'

____

4. 'I did not write half of what I saw, for I knew I would not be believed.'

Genoese navigator – **Christopher Columbus**

Chinese Daoist philosopher – **Lao Tzu**

Italian traveller – **Marco Polo**

English explorer – **Henry Hudson**

Answers on page 176

Fashion Statements

Are these statements about nineteenth- and twentieth-century clothing true or false?

1. The Mao suit, the modern Chinese tunic suit, was invented by Chairman Mao (Mao Zedong).

2. The modern bikini was created partly because of shortages of material following the Second World War.

3. In 1921, Mahatma Gandhi decided to stop wearing Western clothes and only wear simple, traditional Indian clothing because he gave all his money away and could no longer afford Western clothes.

4. Christian Dior's groundbreaking fashion collection in 1947 became known as the Last Look.

5. Blue jeans were invented by Levi Strauss in 1873.

6. During the Second World War, Britain introduced a brand of government-approved basic clothing without frills or extra flourishes, aimed at saving material. It was called the Utility brand.

7. The Edwardian so-called 'health' corset gave women an 'S' shape when viewed from the side.

8. Nylon stockings were invented in Mexico in 1939.

9. Coco Chanel invented the 'little black dress' in 1926.

10. Bloomers, the first trousers widely worn by women in the Western world, were named after the women's activist Amelia Jenks Bloomer.

Answers on page 176

A Crucial Battle

This is a simplified diagram of which important attack during the Second World War? What were its consequences?

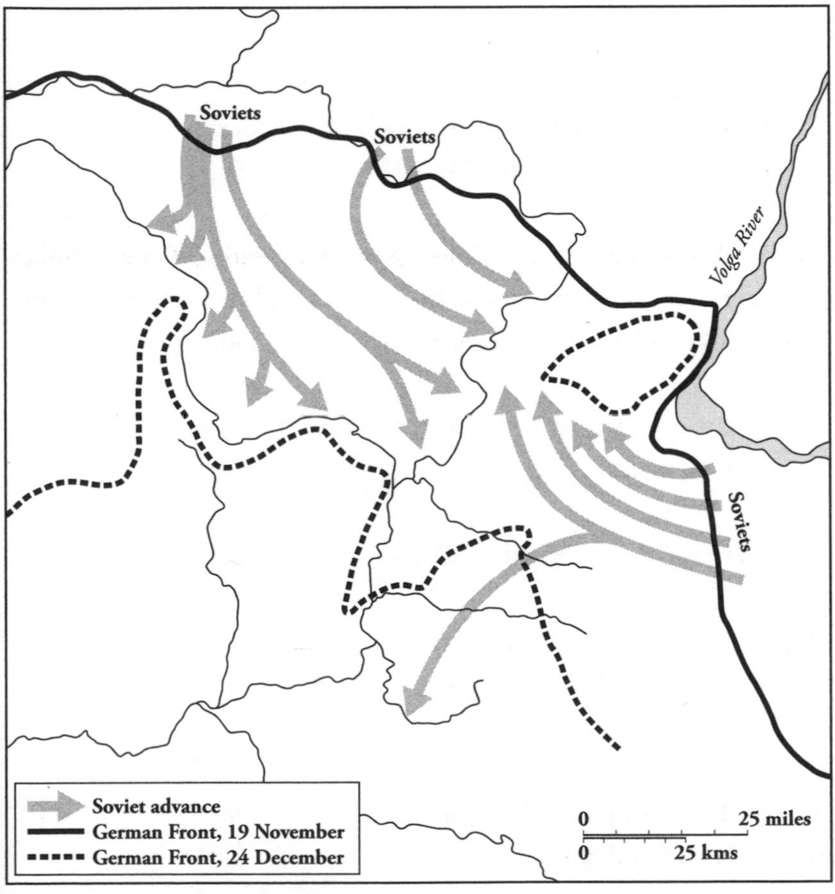

Answers on pages 176-7

Invaders and Dictators

What links:

The Nazis in 1930s' Germany
The Arab conquerors of Alexandria in AD 646
Qin Shi Huangdi, the first emperor of China in 212 BC
Savonarolo of Florence in 1497
The invaders of Nineveh in 612 BC

Table Manners

In terms of personal use for eating, which was invented first, chopsticks, forks, or spoons?

Answers on page 177

What's in a Name?

These people either changed their names or are usually known by a different name or title.

What are their alternative names?

1. **Temüjin Borjigin**
2. **Arthur Wellesley**
3. **Josip Broz**
4. **Ras Tafari**
5. **Joseph Dzhugashvili (Ioseb Besarionis dze Jughashvili)**

New World Map

After the First World War, several new countries were formed. **Which one of these was not a new post-war state?**

Czechoslovakia
Estonia
Finland
Iraq
Romania
Yugoslavia

Answers on page 177

Charles the Great

Charlemagne was the towering figure of Early Medieval Western Europe. He became King of the Franks in AD 768, King of the Lombards in 774, and in 800 the pope gave him another title.

What title was that?

Royal Carpenter

Which European monarch worked as a shipbuilding carpenter, supposedly incognito, while on a tour of other European countries in the late seventeenth century?

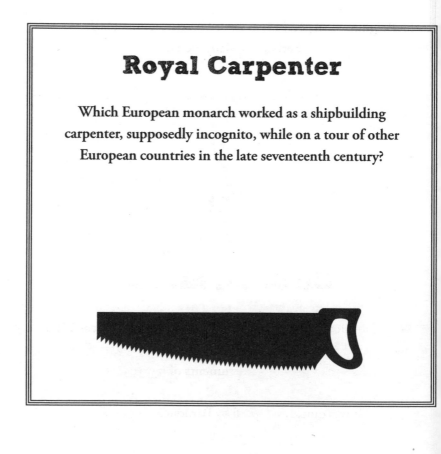

Answers on page 177

Library List

The Scottish-American industrialist and philanthropist Andrew Carnegie donated money to build 2,811 free public libraries, mostly in America. But Carnegie libraries were also built around the world.

Which one of these countries did not have a Carnegie library?

Belgium, Canada, Fiji, France, Mauritius, New Zealand, Serbia, Sweden, the UK

Classical Music

Which musical instrument was invented around the year 1700 and offered a more expressive and controllable range of sound than previous instruments of its type?

It was quickly adopted by Baroque composers.

Answers on page 178

Silhouettes

Identify these buildings or monuments and place them in the order in which they were created:

1. The Easter Island statues
2. The Taj Mahal, India
3. The Eiffel Tower, Paris
4. The heyday of Native Canadian totem poles
5. The Colosseum, Rome
6. Stonehenge, England
7. The Great Wall of China
8. Peru's Nazca Plain Lines
9. The Great Pyramid, Egypt
10. The cathedral Sagrada Familia, Barcelona

Answers on page 178

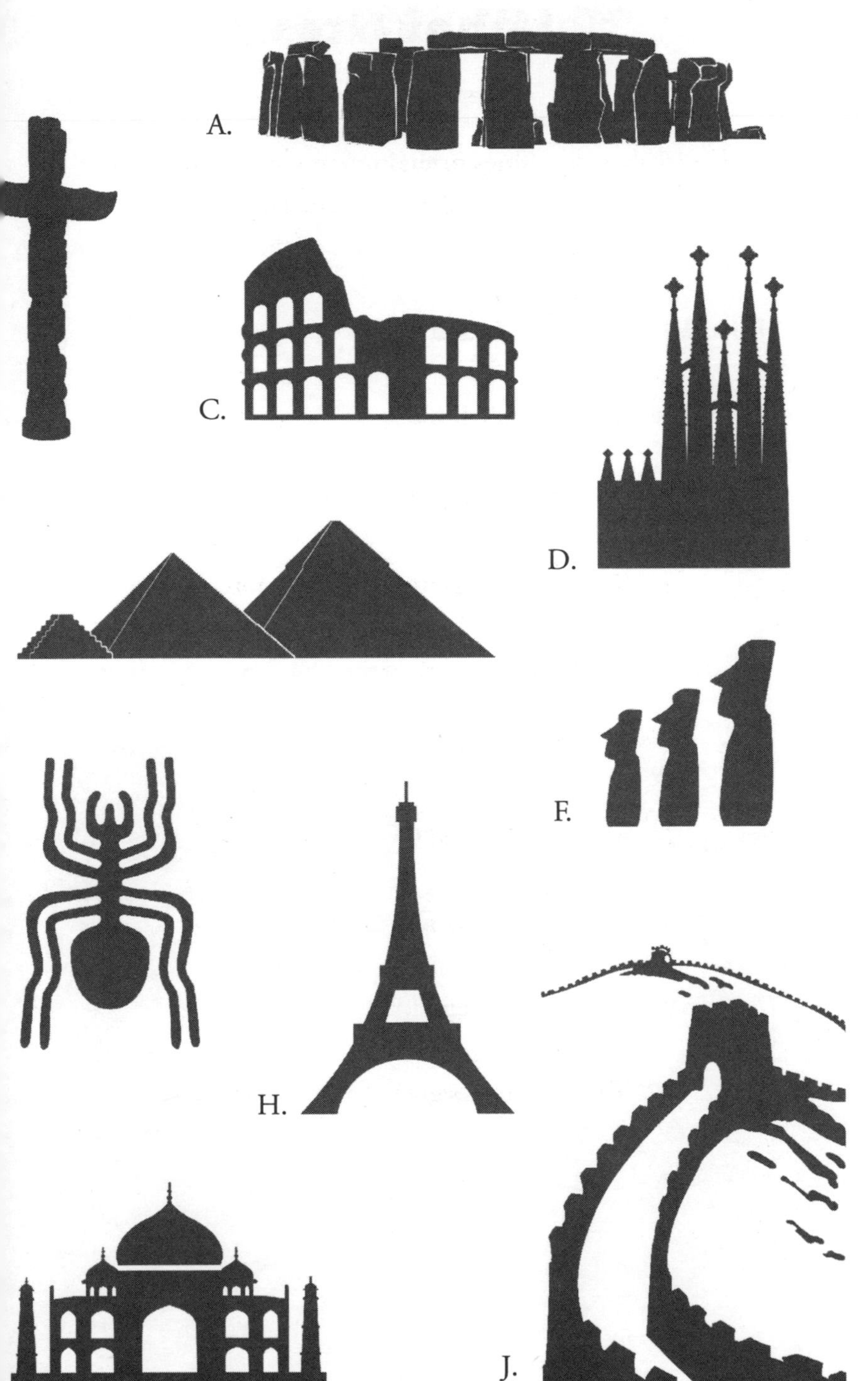
A.
C.
D.
F.
H.
J.

National Growth

Through what different means did these nations expand their territories?

1. The Dutch Republic (the Netherlands) in the seventeenth century

2. Britain's Canadian colonies in 1759

3. The USA in 1803

Europe in 1812

What do each of the four shaded areas of this map represent?

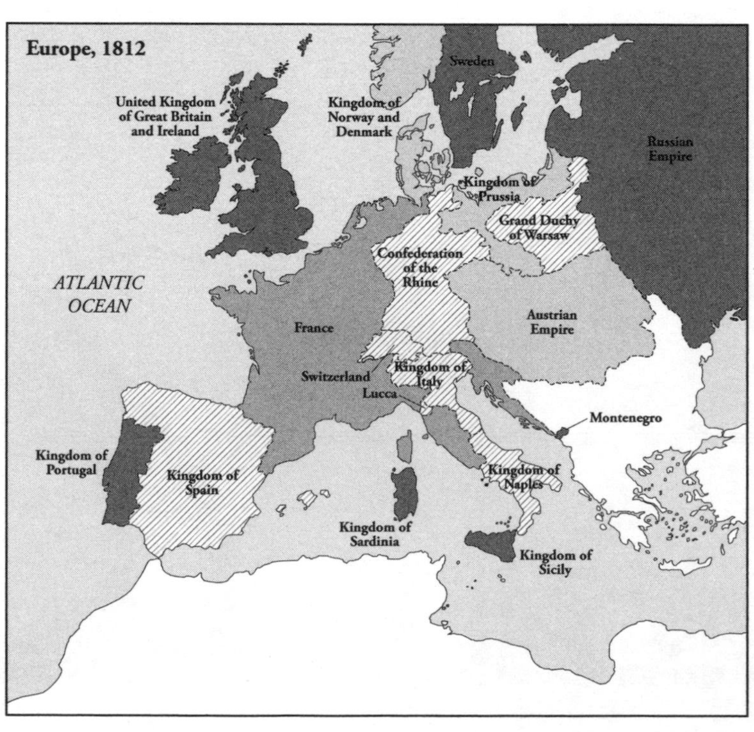

Answers on pages 178-9

Historical Quotes

Match the person to the quote they wrote or said:

1. *'History is the version of past events that people have decided to agree upon.'*

2. *'History repeats itself, first as tragedy, second as farce.'*

3. *'Let others praise ancient times; I am glad I was born in these.'*

4. *'If you think in terms of a year, plant a seed; if in terms of ten years, plant trees; if in terms of 100 years, teach the people.'*

5. *'… leave the past to history, especially as I propose to write that history.'*

A. Confucius
B. Roman poet Ovid
C. Winston Churchill
D. Karl Marx
E. Napoleon Bonaparte

Answers on page 179

Italy Before Unification

Before Italy was unified into the Kingdom of Italy in 1861, the country was a patchwork of small kingdoms, republics and other states.

Which one of these was not an Italian state that became part of the new nation?

Kingdom of Naples
Republic of Venice
Duchy of Milan
Bolognese Principality
Grand Duchy of Tuscany
Papal States
Duchy of Savoy

Significant Others

Who were the husbands of these women:

1. **Nefertiti of Egypt**
2. **Roxana of Central Asia**
3. **Eleanor of Aquitaine**
4. **Elizabeth I of England**
5. **Mumtaz Mahal of India**
6. **Marie Curie**

Answers on page 179

War and Peace

Who wrote or said these quotes:

1. *'Don't fire until you see the whites of their eyes!'*

2. *'I will fight no more forever.'*

3. *'Today the guns are silent. A great tragedy has ended. A great victory has been won.'*

4. *'The Greatest Happiness is to scatter your enemy and drive him before you. To see his cities reduced to ashes. To see those who love him shrouded and in tears.'*

A. Genghis Khan
B. Second World War U.S. General Douglas MacArthur
C. American Revolutionary Colonel William Prescott
D. Native American Nez Perce leader Chief Joseph

Answers on page 180

Dot to Dot

Join the dots to reveal a mysterious ancient construction.

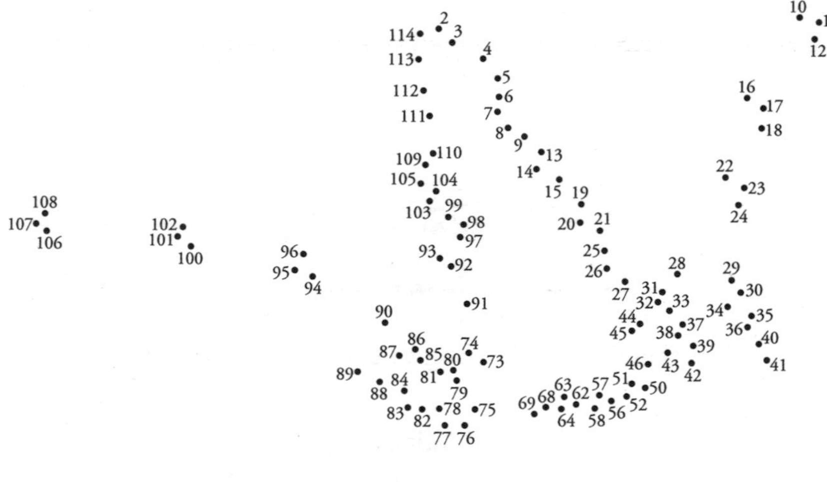

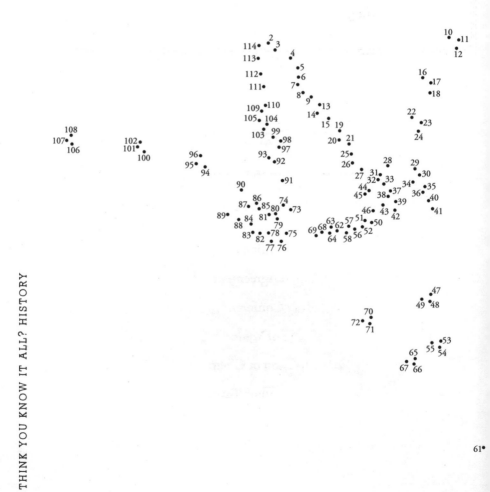

Answer on pages 180

Artistic Order

Arrange these works of art, monuments or buildings in the order in which they were created:

1. The *Mona Lisa* by Leonardo da Vinci
2. *The Scream* by Edvard Munch
3. The Pyramid of the Sun, Teotihuacan, Mexico
4. *Sunflowers* by Vincent van Gogh
5. Edinburgh Castle
6. Ming vases

Odd One Out

Which of these international agreements is the odd one out?

Auld Alliance

Munich Agreement

Solvay Conference

Peace of Venice

Pacification of Ghent

Convention of Turin

Answers on page 181

American Presidents

Place these American presidents in chronological order:

1. Theodore Roosevelt
2. George Washington
3. Ulysses S. Grant
4. Dwight D. Eisenhower
5. Franklin D. Roosevelt
6. Abraham Lincoln

Linked In

What is the link between:

The ancient Greek general Alcibiades

The English Princes in the Tower

The Mexican revolutionary Pancho Villa

The German socialist Rosa Luxemburg

Answers on page 181

An English Maze

This is a maze created with hedges between 1689 and 1695 which still stands in a palatial English garden.

Can you find your way into its centre and then out again?

And which existing maze do you think it is?

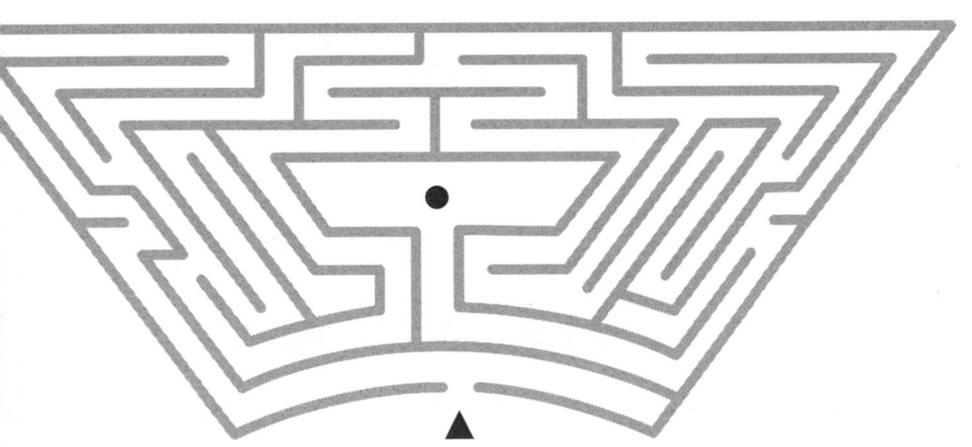

Answers on page 182

Traditions

Name the countries or regions in which these cultural traditions evolved or with which they are most associated:

1. Noh theatre
2. Shadow puppets
3. Harlequin
4. Clog dancing
5. Djembe drumming
6. Bagpipes
7. The cancan
8. Ceremonies at the base of Uluru

Initial Values

What do these twentieth-century initials stand for?

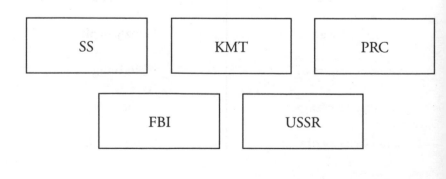

SS	KMT	PRC
FBI	USSR	

Answers on page 182

Teetotal Years

From 1920 to 1933 alcohol was banned in the USA.

What name was given to this period?

Before the ban, there were about 15,000 drinking saloons in New York City.

During the ban, how many illegal 'speakeasies' serving alcohol were there in that city alone?

A. 3,200
B. 15,000
C. 32,000

Dynasty

Match these empires or dynasties to their founders:

Assyria	**Manco Capac**
Inca	**Franz Joseph**
Guptan empire of India	**Liu Bang**
Austria-Hungary	**Chandra**
Han dynasty of China	**Ashur-uballit**

Answers on page 183

What's the Link?

What links:

A. Julius Caesar, Pope Gregory XIII and Kemal Ataturk?

B. Pudding Lane, London; Mother O'Leary's cow, Chicago; Roman general Scipio Aemilianus in North Africa; and a cursed Japanese kimono in Edo?

War Production

In 1914, at the start of the First World War, which European country was producing the most steel and coal, products which were vital for industry and twentieth-century warfare?

Answers on page 183

Artistic Time Travel

You decide to use your time machine to visit some of the great artistic and musical moments of the past. Once again, you can only go backwards once, and then forwards in time until you come home. So, you need to plan your visits from the earliest through to the most recent.

Sort these magical moments into their chronological order:

A. The Harlem Renaissance
B. The Founding of the Pre-Raphaelite Brotherhood
C. The heyday of Benin bronzes
D. Chartres Cathedral is finished in France
E. A Shang Dynasty bronze vessel being crafted in China
F. Beethoven completed his *Moonlight Sonata*

Answers on pages 183-4

Football Pictogram

Which twentieth-century event does this represent?

Answer on page 184

Missing Words

Fill in the gaps in this story:

Once upon a time there lived a king called Mansa _____ . He ruled over the magnificent Empire of Mali in _____ Africa, to the south of the _____ Desert. The empire was wealthy because of its trade in several things, including a mineral that is essential to life, _____ . The city of Timbuktu, a great centre of learning, became part of the kingdom of Mali and also thrived on an unusual trade, in _____ . The emperor followed the religion of _____ , and in 1324 he undertook the Hajj, or pilgrimage to _____ . Thousands of people travelled in his entourage, which included animals such as camels and _____ that were well known in Africa but were quite exotic in Arabia, and could carry many people at a time.

The emperor was one of the wealthiest people in history, because he extended the empire and during his reign it probably produced more _____ than any other country at the time. This is a yellow metal that has been valued in every country and in every period of history.

The emperor was generous to everyone, giving alms to poor people and presents to the many dignitaries he met along the way and to the cities that he visited. Along with the money, he left a trail of wonder behind him.

The emperor became well known in North Africa and the Middle East because of his awesome pilgrimage. The news also spread to the northern Mediterranean. As a result, Mali was included in the Catalan Atlas, a map of the _____ made in 1375 in the country of _____ . The emperor was also later visited by the Arab traveller and historian Ibn B_____ .

Answers on page 184

A Common Wealth

Name the six self-governing colonies that federated into the Commonwealth of Australia in 1901.

1.
2.
3.
4.
5.
6.

Which British colony decided not to unite with them?

Money Talks

Before the First World War the highest-denomination German banknote was 1,000 marks.

After the hyperinflation in the early 1920s, what was the highest-denomination banknote in 1923?

A. 5,000 marks
B. 1 million marks
C. 500 million marks

Answers on page 184

Scientific Exile

Which one of these scientists did not flee from Nazi Germany or Austria because they had Jewish ancestry?

Albert Einstein
Werner Heisenberg
Lise Meitner
Erwin Schrödinger
Otto Stern
Leo Szilard

Answer on page 184

Life is Better With …

Can you put these everyday twentieth-century items in the order in which they were invented?

1. Nylon
2. The modern backless bra
3. The roadside cat's eye reflector
4. Cornflakes
5. The Model T Ford motor car

Answers on page 185

An Ancient Maze

This is a type of maze found in several ancient cultures. In classical tradition this sort of maze was meant to imprison a half-human, half-bull monster.

1. What is this type of maze known as?

2. Although this type of maze can be found in many countries, which classical civilization had this tradition of the imprisoned monster within the maze?

3. What was the creature called?

4. What object, typical of that culture, did the maze's name probably derive from? Can you find a way into the centre of the maze?

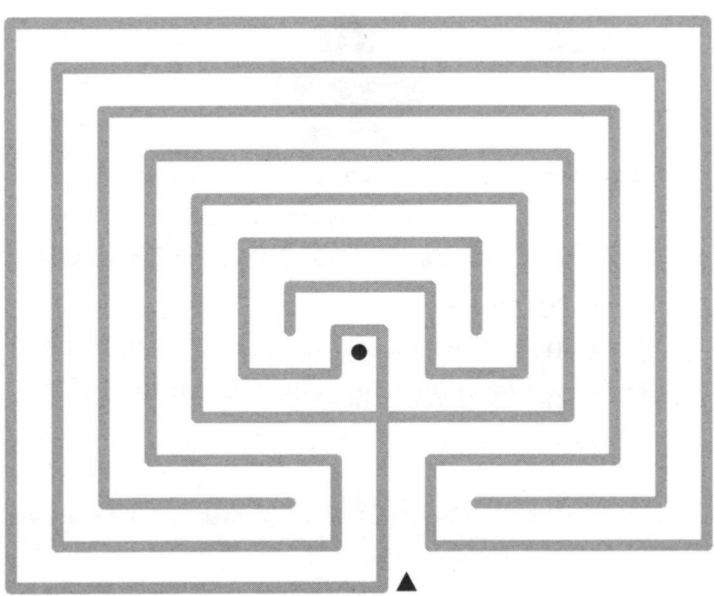

Answers on page 185

A Novel Approach to History

List these historical works of literature in the order in which they were written, and describe the historical period in which the stories are set.

A. *The Three Musketeers* by Alexandre Dumas

B. *The Red Badge of Courage* by Stephen Crane

C. *War and Peace* by Leo Tolstoy

D. *Romance of the Three Kingdoms* by Luo Guanzhong

E. *A Tale of Two Cities* by Charles Dickens

Canadian Confederation

What were the three British colonies that united in the confederation of the Dominion of Canada in 1867?

Which colony then immediately divided into two new provinces, and what were they called?

Answers on page 186

Thirty Years of Terror

1. One of these was not a factor in the Thirty Years War of 1618–48. Which one?

A. Rivalry between the Habsburg and Wittelsbach families, the two most powerful dynasties in the Holy Roman Empire

B. States' desire to expand their territories and prominence in international affairs

C. Disputes over the division of wealth from the Americas

D. Religious conflict between Catholics and Protestants

2. In what nation was the Thirty Years War fought?

3. Which two foreign countries also played a major part in the Thirty Years War?

4. Following the Thirty Years War, which country became the dominant European nation for nearly two centuries?

Answers on page 186

Natural Disaster

Which twentieth-century natural disaster is shown here?

What man-made causes contributed to it?

Which financial disaster did it exacerbate?

What terrible event brought an end to these economic problems throughout the Western world?

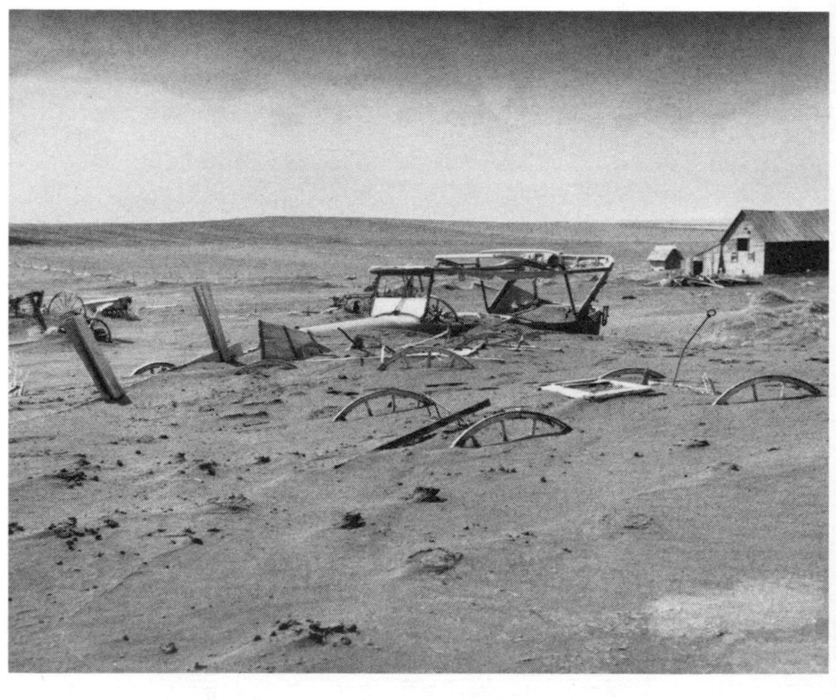

Answers on pages 186-7

The Third Rome

After Constantinople fell to the Ottomans in 1453, which European city was named the 'Third Rome'?

A. Moscow
B. Paris
C. Vienna

Ancient Thinker

Which Greek philosopher tutored the young Alexander of Macedon, founded the original lyceum school, and later fled from Athens, reportedly saying that he would not permit Athens to sin twice against philosophy?

What was he referring to in his statement?

Answers on page 187

Factions

What is the origin of the political terms left-wing and right-wing?

A. After a crucial parliamentary vote before the English Civil Wars of the 1600s, the Royalist supporters turned to the right when leaving the voting chamber.

B. Before the American Revolution, representatives who wanted to remain loyal to Britain gathered on the right-hand side of the meeting place.

C. During the early days of the French Revolution, parliamentary members who supported the royal regime sat together on the right-hand side of the presiding officer.

Death by Every Means Possible

The European conquest of the Americas was brutal. Indigenous inhabitants were killed in warfare, tortured to death and enslaved.

But what decimated their numbers more than any atrocities?

Answers on page 187

First Words

What were the first clearly heard words ever spoken on a telephone?

A. *'I'm on the phone …'*

B. *'Hello, hello? Can you hear me?'*

C. *'Mr Watson, come here. I want to see you.'*

Missing Amenities?

When the French Palace of Versailles was built in the seventeenth century there were not enough toilet facilities, or in those days, commodes. As a result, commodes would overflow and courtiers would relieve themselves in the corners of rooms and corridors, which as a result became somewhat stinky.

True or false?

Answers on page 187

Film Night, Part 2

1. During Nazi-occupied Europe, what was the nationality and ethnic background of the female Resistance spy, featured in Dutch film *Black Book*?

2. The South African science-fiction film *District 9* features aliens who are forced to live in separate districts from humans. It parodies a policy formally introduced in South Africa soon after the Second World War. What was that policy known as and what is its literal meaning?

3. With whom does the personification of Death play a game of chess in which Ingmar Bergman film?

4. In the Hong Kong action film *The Way of the Dragon*, Bruce Lee fights Chuck Norris in what famous historical arena?

5. Japanese anime film-maker Miyazaki Hayao and his Studio Ghibli have produced many fantasy films. But what is the historical subject of his film *The Wind Rises*?

Answers on page 188

Absolute Advances

Marie Theresa of Austria and her son Joseph II were absolute monarchs, yet were more benevolent than several other rulers of the time.

In 1776 which old, barbaric legal practice did they abolish?

And in 1781, which social class did Joseph abolish?

A Gap in the Map

1. Which Eastern European country was a powerful medieval state, united with Lithuania in 1386, then was annexed and partitioned by Russia, Prussia and Austria, and disappeared as an independent country until after the First World War?

2. This country produced Jan III Sobieski, who was acclaimed as a hero for what feat?

A. He defeated the Ottomans at the siege of Vienna in 1683

B. He defeated the Wallachian warlord Vlad the Impaler

C. He distributed food during a widespread famine

Answers on page 188

Missing Treasures

This might be a tricky question for some people, but it will suit treasure-hunters and lovers of Indiana Jones. Over time, many precious items or whole treasure troves have been lost or stolen, never to be seen again.

Can you match the numbered routes that lead to these lost treasures and identify them from the clues?

A. Regalia stolen in 1907 from Dublin Castle in Ireland
B. A traditional national icon of Japan, the H__ M__, lost after the Second World War
C. A jeweller's masterpieces, several of which went missing in the early nineteenth century

Answers on page 188

School's Out For Some

Nicholas I became Russian tsar in 1825. Under his rule, which classes of people were allowed to go to secondary schools and universities?

A. Everyone except serfs

B. Only the nobility

C. Everyone except serfs, children from merchant families and the children of blacksmiths

Age of Discovery

In 1498, which European nation was the first to reach India by sea, later reached Japan by sea and established trading posts in India, China, Malaysia and throughout South East Asia?

But this country was too small to attempt to conquer Asian countries, and in the end lost most of its advantages there to another small European country.

What was this other small European country that gained the advantage in Asia?

Answers on page 188

Industrial Reasons

There were several reasons why the Industrial Revolution began in Britain around 1750.

Which one of these is not true?

A. Britain had had a stable government and society for some time

B. Although Britain had been involved in several wars, it did not suffer a serious invasion and major fighting – and therefore terrible social disruption – on its own soil

C. It was very difficult to transport goods and materials through the British countryside, so inventors and engineers had to come up with new means of transport

D. There was a plentiful supply of coal, the fuel of choice for early industry

Dancing Years

In which country and century did the forms of classical ballet develop?

A. France in the late eighteenth century

B. Italy in the early nineteenth century

C. Russia in the late nineteenth century

Answers on page 189

Spot the Difference

Who is this twentieth-century statesman?

Find ten differences between the first and second picture.

One of the changes in the second picture is an anachronism. What is it?

Answers on page 189

Literate History

Which one of these books matches the description of it, or a description that is often applied to it or the author, and who wrote the books?

(Some of the titles are abridged)

'The first novel'	*Divine Comedy*	Johann Wolfgang von Goe
'The first modern novel'	*The Lord of the Rings*	Gustave Flaubert
'The first science-fiction novel'	*Faust*	Fyodor Dostoyevsky
'Masterpiece of Realism'	*Crime and Punishment*	Mary Shelley
'Greatest writer in the English language'	*Life of Frederick Douglass*	J.R.R. Tolkien
Influential slave narrative	*Madame Bovary*	Miguel de Cervantes
Italian epic poem	*The Tale of Genji*	Dante Alighieri
'Greatest work in the German language'	*Complete Works*	Frederick Douglass
'Nihilism, damnation, redemption'	*Don Quixote*	William Shakespeare
Foundation of modern fantasy	*Frankenstein*	Murasaki Shikibu

Answers on page 190

Mass Marketing

In 1916 the U.S. Rubber Company created an offshoot, Keds, to mass-market an item that previously not everyone could afford. Their product became wildly popular, was quickly copied by competitors, and can now be found on most streets in the world.

What did Keds introduce?

What did they become known as in America, and why?

Answers on page 190

Buy and Sell

Where was the world's first stock exchange founded in 1602?

A. Amsterdam
B. London
C. New York

Answer on page 191

Taxing Times

1. What did Peter the Great of Russia tax in 1698 in his attempts to 'Westernize' Russian customs?

2. In 1930 Mahatma Gandhi led a protest march against a British law taxing which substance in India? Tax on this substance was also so unpopular in France that it contributed to the French Revolution.

3. In 1696, what part of a building did England tax, leading to odd-looking houses and eventually to a health problem that caused the tax to be revoked?

4. In ancient Egypt tax collectors would make surprise visits to households to check which common cooking substance had been properly taxed?

5. What was the name of the act that taxed newspapers, legal documents and all printed papers in Britain's American colonies, leading to protests that helped bring about the American Revolution?

Give and Take

In 1884 the Canadian and U.S. governments banned a practice that was common amongst the Native groups along the Northwest coast. It involved a lot of conspicuous consumption, gift-giving and deliberate destruction of valuable goods.

What was it called?

Answers on page 191

Dutch Division

In 1831 which country became independent of the Netherlands?

Ancient Wonders

What were the Seven Wonders of the Ancient World, and which ones still stand today?

1.
2.
3.
4.
5.
6.
7.

Answers on page 191

A Rather Expensive Child Support Bill

About 8 per cent of men from Central and East Asia carry a certain Y-chromosome that is thought to have come down the generations from just one fearsome – and clearly prolific – individual. This amounts to many millions of descendants.

Who was their ancestor?

Waste Not

Up until the 1920s a by-product of the oil industry was burnt off as waste. Then, engineers realized that it was a valuable fuel in its own right.

What is it?

Answers on page 191

D-Day Beaches

1. Can you give the date of D-Day, the invasion of Normandy that began the process of freeing Europe from the Nazis?

2. What were the code names of the five landing beaches chosen for the invasion?

3. Which of the Allies led the assaults on the different beaches?

4. Apart from the seaborne assaults on beaches, there were two further Allied assaults on D-Day, marked A and B on the map. Which troops conducted these?

5. Although the majority of the invasion troops were from the countries that led the assaults on the beaches, many soldiers, sailors and airmen from several other nations took part in D-Day. Can you name at least three other nationalities who fought in the invasion?

6. What were the Allied operational names for the Normandy invasion and for the landing operations?

7. Who was the overall Allied commander, and what position did he take up in 1953?

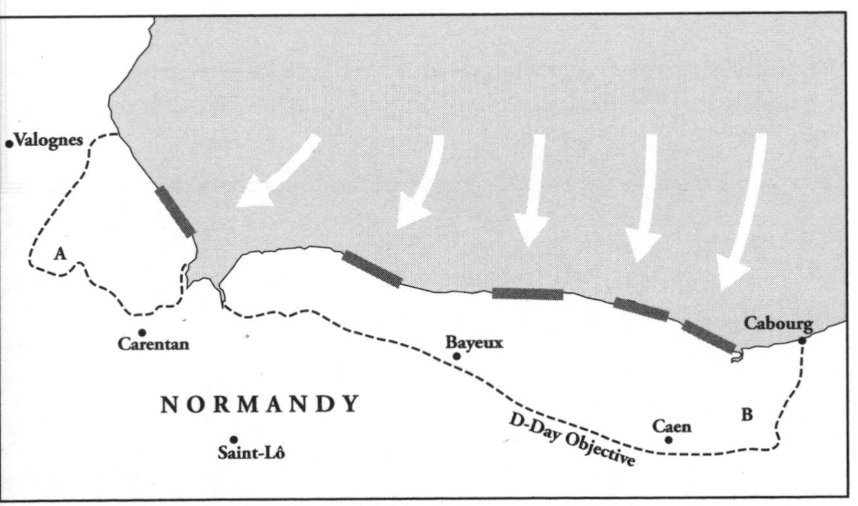

Answers on page 192

Links Across Time

What links the ancient Greek scientist Archimedes, the ancient Greek king Agamemnon and French revolutionary Jean-Paul Marat?

Everyday Items

In 1596 Englishman Sir John Harington built what is considered to be the first modern one. The Romans had shared ones. A 2,000-year-old one was found in a Han Chinese archaeological site and there were versions in ancient Egypt, the Indus Valley cities and Stone-Age Orkney.

What were they?

Answers on page 193

Right to Rule

Who was the last hereditary monarch to rule France, and what happened to him or her?

Oldest Event

Which one of these events did not happen in the twentieth century?

A. The Japanese navy defeated Russia at the Battle of Tsushima

B. The Taiping Rebellion began in China

C. Norway separated from Sweden

D. The Portuguese Revolution ended the monarchy in Portugal

E. The Union of South Africa was formed by the Cape Colony, the Natal Colony, the Orange River Colony, and the Transvaal

Answers on page 193

Escapees

What was the main provision of the Fugitive Slave Act that was passed by the U.S. Congress in 1850?

A. State officials were required to help capture runaway slaves and return them to the slave-owner

B. Runaway slaves were permanently free if they reached a state where slavery was illegal

C. Runaway slaves were given a small sum of money to help them settle in the free states

Industrial Expansion

Which was the second part of the world to embark upon the Industrial Revolution after Britain?

A Royal Fleet

During the seventeenth-century English Civil Wars, Prince Rupert of the Rhine became commander of the Royalist fleet.

In order to raise funds, what did he resort to?

Answers on page 193

Russian Rulers

In 1613 a tsar from a new ruling family was chosen to become Russian emperor. His descendants would rule until the Revolution of 1917.

What was his family name?

Answer on page 193

A Common Touch, Part 2

What did the following men have in common?

American Civil War General **William Tecumseh Sherman**

Holy Roman Emperor **Frederick I (Frederick Barbarossa)**

Viking explorer **Leif Erikson**, son of Erik the Red

The Ottoman pirate and naval commander **Hayreddin Barbarossa**

Hugh Roe O'Donnell, also known as 'Red Hugh', one of the leaders of the rebellion against English rule in Ireland in 1593

Answer on page 194

A Timeline

Which ancient civilization had a counting system based on 60 rather than 10, so gave us an hour with 60 minutes and a minute with 60 seconds?

A. Greek
B. Chinese
C. Babylonian

Terracotta Tomb

As well as the soldiers of the Terracotta Army in China, several other types of figures were buried in the tomb, including animals.

What was the most common animal?

A. Horses
B. Pandas
C. Camels

How many figures overall have so far been found in the Terracotta Army?

A. 700 people, animals and chariots
B. Around 1,000 people, animals and chariots
C. More than 7,000 people, animals and chariots

Answers on page 194

First Fascists

Which sector of society was most supportive of the early fascist movements in Italy and Germany after the First World War?

A. War veterans
B. War widows
C. War orphans

Revolutionary Slaves

Where was the only revolt by enslaved people in the Americas that led to an independent state?

When was it, and which successful general, a leading light of the rebellion, was betrayed and died in captivity before independence was achieved?

Global Link

What links the Indian Mughal Emperor Akbar, Shah Abbas the Great of Persia, Queen Elizabeth I of England and Tsar Boris Godunov of Russia?

Answers on page 194

Post-War Changes

After the Second World War devastated countries and economies, there were some drastic changes.

1. **Who emerged from the war with the world's strongest economy?**

2. **What was the only Eastern European country that was not dominated by the Soviet Union after the war?**

3. **Which Asian country gained its independence from Britain in 1947 but divided into two?**

4. **What Middle Eastern country was founded in 1948?**

Pre-Revolutionary Times

What were the Three Estates that were represented in the French parliament before the Revolution?

And which two sections of society did not have to pay taxes?

Answers on page 194

Shared Experiences

What childhood experience did Attila the Hun share with Tokugawa Ieyasu, the first Tokugawa shogun of Japan, and Vlad the Impaler and his brother Radu?

If this seems too tricky, then consider the following people who experienced the same but as adults:

Theodoric the Great of the Ostrogoths
King James I of Scotland

If you would like a further clue, then the following people shared part of the experience when adults, but for a different reason:

Julius Caesar
Richard I of England (the Lionheart)
Spanish writer Miguel de Cervantes
Chinese Nationalist leader Chiang Kai-shek

City Links

Which European city is historically linked with ghettoes, quarantine and masks?

Answers on pages 194-5

Year of Revolution

1. When was the Year of Revolution in Europe, also known as the Spring of Nations?

2. In which five countries did the most significant revolutions take place?

3. Which country saw a massive public meeting that terrified the authorities, but which turned into a peaceful picnic instead of an uprising?

4. Which revolutionary pamphlet was published that year and become one of the world's most important political documents?

Ten Thousand or Two?

Which Asian ruler boasted that his family would rule for ten thousand generations but the dynasty did not last two generations?

Answers on page 195

Criminal Conference

What was the outcome of the Wannsee Conference?

Assassinated Presidents

Before 1950, which American presidents were assassinated, and when?
Which relative of the first assassinated president was present,
or very nearly on the spot, for all of the murders?

1.

2.

3.

Answers on page 196

What Links?

What links the cities of Dublin in Ireland, Oslo in Norway, Novgorod in Russia and the Duchy of Normandy in France?

Maori Customs

From the late eighteenth century onwards, European and American ships regularly visited New Zealand and islands in the South Pacific. Many of these sailors returned home with a 'souvenir' of their travels, something that had been a long-standing Maori and South Pacific cultural tradition.

What was it?

Little Wonder

A working model of which small device, which would go on to revolutionize electronics, was first made in 1947?

Answers on page 196

Who Was She?

Having escaped from slavery in the Southern American states, she risked everything by returning South about thirteen times to guide some seventy runaway slaves to freedom in the North, and later to Canada. She is reported to have pulled a gun on an escapee who wanted to turn back, saying, 'You go on or die.' During the American Civil War she was a spy and scout for the Union, and became the first woman in the war to lead an armed raid.

Korean Conquest

Which country conquered Korea in 1910 and ruled it until 1945?

First Colony

Where was the first English colony in North America?

A. Roanoke Island off North Carolina
B. St John's, Newfoundland
C. Plymouth Colony, Massachusetts

Answers on page 196

Mongol Maze

Oh, no! You are peacefully shepherding your sheep in medieval Central Asia and you see a horde of Mongol warriors coming your way. It is up to you to raise the alarm back at your village so you can all run away to safety in the mountains. Will you get to your village in time? It depends on which path you choose. The distance between you and the Mongols will remain the same unless you hit barriers or find an advantage. Hills will slow you down. But, although you are on foot and the Mongols are on horseback, the Mongols will have to go slowly in a meadow full of rabbit burrows or their horses will trip up. Additionally, you can run in the narrow gap between trees in a wood, where horses won't fit. So if you can find a path that avoids hills you will reach the village in time.

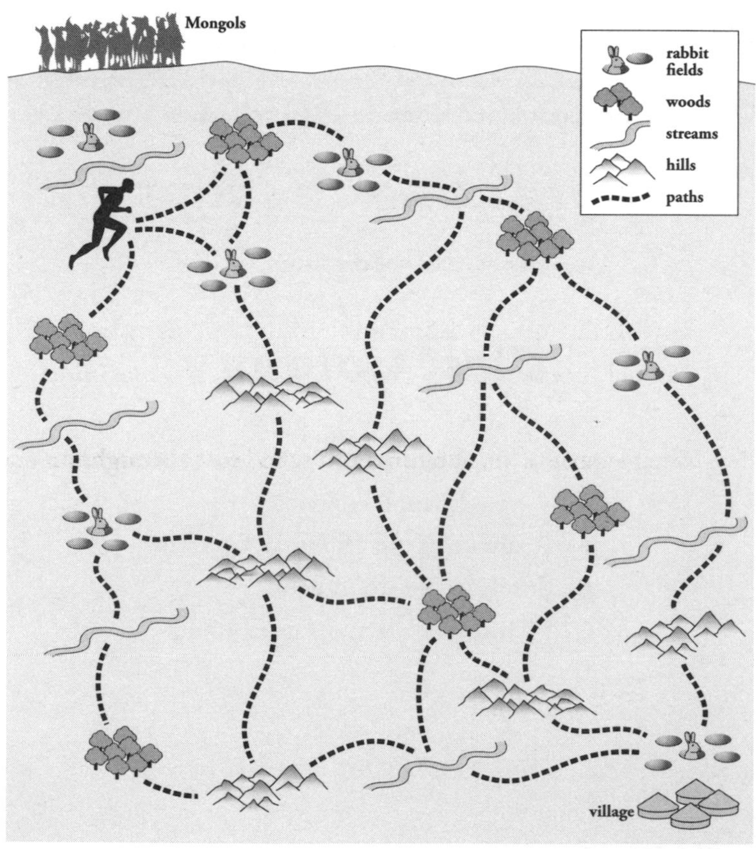

Answers on pages 196-197

A Rare Defeat

Who suffered a rare but decisive defeat at the Battle of the Catalaunian Plains in AD 451?

Who were the victors?

Byzantine Factions

In the early Middle Ages, the Byzantine Empire regularly saw rioting by and fights between huge mobs divided into two factions.

What was the basis of the factions, and what event brought an end to the mob violence?

Answers on page 197

Jamaican Heroine

What name is given to the communities of escaped enslaved Africans and native Taino people who evaded the Spanish and British rulers of Jamaica?

Who was the woman leader of one of those communities who devised guerrilla tactics to resist the British soldiers? She was given a royal title out of respect for her achievements.

Land Grab

In 1913 the South African government set a certain amount of land aside solely for white settlers.

What percentage of the country's land was it?

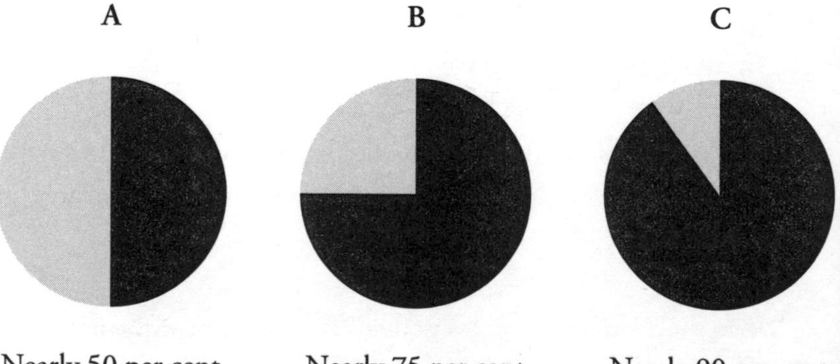

Nearly 50 per cent | Nearly 75 per cent | Nearly 90 per cent

Answers on page 198

The Dealer

What did President Theodore Roosevelt promise America?

A. A Square Deal
B. A Raw Deal
C. A Fair Deal

A Canadian Home

Around the year AD 1000, who lived at L'Anse aux Meadows in Newfoundland, Canada?

Advertising

In 1949 the last four letters, spelling 'land', were taken off a large advertising sign promoting real estate in a Californian city.

What word was left on the sign, which is now one of the most famous in the world?

Answers on page 198

People of the Year

Since 1927, *Time* magazine has featured a 'Person of the Year'. While this is meant to just acknowledge people who have had the biggest impact on the news during the year, it is held by many to be a personal honour. During the 1930s, some of history's worst dictators were named *Time*'s people of the year, along with one of the world's great peacemakers, politicians and a woman who brought down a king.

Can you name *Time's* ten people of the year from 1930 to 1939?

1.

2.

3.

4.

5.

6.

7.

8.

9.

10.

Answers on page 198

Get Ahead

Which ancient American culture created these giant heads?

A. Toltec
B. Olmec
C. Aztec
D. Inca

First Things First

Up until around 1400, what was the most technologically advanced country in the world?

Can you name three things that were first invented in this country before 1400?

Answers on pages 198-9

Who Were They?

Which civilization is this?

They had no alphabetic writing
They used knots in strings for keeping records and for communication
They used wheels only on children's toys
They had an extensive road network

What were the knots known as?

Six Degrees of Separation

Connect medieval traveller Marco Polo to the Elizabethan English playwright William Shakespeare through a chain of six links or 'degrees of separation'.

Now connect the two with just one link.

____

____

____

____

____

____

Answers on page 199

An Americas Sequence

What is this sequence that took place in the late fifteenth and early sixteenth centuries?

The Bahamas

Cuba

Hispaniola (Haiti and the Dominican Republic)

Virgin Islands

Puerto Rico

Jamaica

Trinidad

Venezuela

Panama

Answers on page 199

First Writings

Identify these early forms of writing and the countries they originated in:

A.

B.

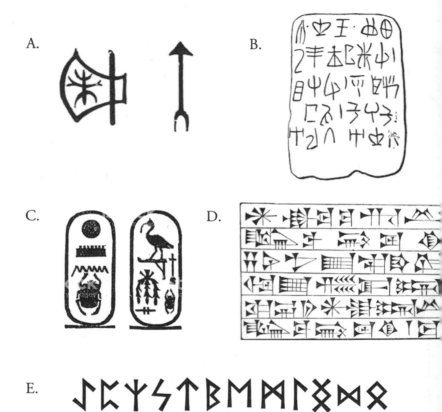

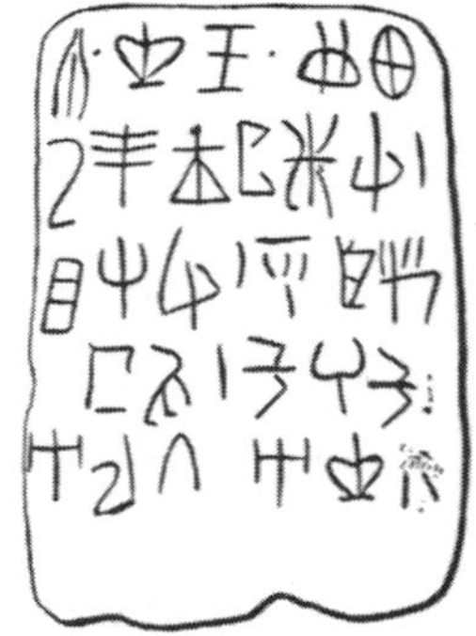

C.

D.

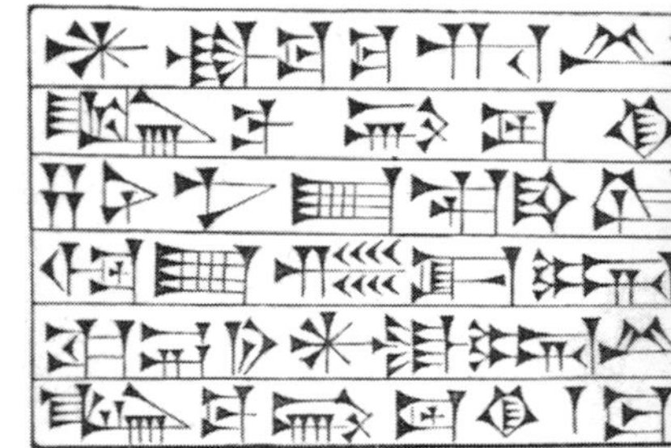

E. ᛇᛈᛉᛊᛏᛒᛗᛞᛚᛝᛞᛟ

F.

What links B and F ?

Answers on pages 199-200

Resistance Was Not Futile

In support of the D-Day landings in the Second World War, the French Resistance carried out widespread sabotage to hinder German troop movements.

Which one of these actions did they not undertake?

A. Attempted to assassinate Hitler
B. Sabotaged the rail network
C. Cut telephone lines

How were the Allied plans for D-Day conveyed to the Resistance?

A. Carrier pigeon
B. Coded messages broadcast by the BBC
C. Instruction codes in love letters posted to Resistance members

Who Said?

Who said 'I am just going outside and may be some time'?

When, and on what occasion?

Answers on page 200

Odd One Out: North American Battles

Which of these battles that took place in North America is the odd one out?

A. Cold Harbor
B. Cedar Creek
C. Guilford Court House
D. Yellow Tavern

Non-Combatants

Apart from the usual baggage-train of cooks, servants, etc, which particular types of non-combatants marched with these armies?

1. The ancient Assyrians
2. Alexander the Great
3. The Romans

Answers on page 200

Zones of Influence

At the end of the Second World War, Germany was split into four separate zones each run by one of the Allies.

1. Which countries administered the zones?

2. In whose zone did Berlin lie and which of the Allies administered the city?

3. What happened in that city in 1948–9?

Successful Sisters

In AD 40 the Trung sisters, Trung Trac and Trung Nhj, led a successful (if not particularly long-lived) rebellion against Chinese control of which country?

Answers on pages 200-1

Toy Stories

What is the earliest known picture of a yo-yo?

A. A painting on an ancient Greek vase
B. A sketch by Leonardo da Vinci
C. An advert in a small Midwest American newspaper in 1905

Where did the earliest known toy made of an animal sliding down a string or a rod come from? And which animal was it?

A. The Indus Valley civilization of Pakistan and India – a monkey
B. The Dutch Golden Age as merchants explored Africa and Asia – a parrot
C. Victorian Britain as the Industrial Revolution led to new manufacturing opportunities – a cat

Who is the teddy bear named after?

Answers on page 201

Successful Strategy

What was the German name widely applied to the Nazis' military tactic that they used successfully in the Second World War, particularly in the 1940 invasions of Belgium, the Netherlands and France?

How does this translate, and what did it involve?

Name That Year

These events all took place in the same year. What was it?

It was Albert Einstein's annus mirabilis or 'miracle year' when he published four groundbreaking physics papers, including one on special relativity

The Fauvist art movement began

The provinces of Alberta and Saskatchewan were founded in the west of Canada

There was a mutiny aboard the Russian battleship *Potemkin*

Answers on page 201

An African Queen

Who was the seventeenth-century African queen in what is now Angola who led resistance against the Portuguese through guerrilla warfare and local alliances?

A. Nzinga
B. Cleopatra
C. Ashanta

Last Outpost

Apart from quite small islands, what was the last country in the world to be inhabited by human beings, and approximately when?

From where did those settlers travel?

Answers on page 201

A Growing Question

Identify these five flowers and plants and match them to their picture:

1. A flower that caused an economic 'mania' in a European country, possibly the first ever speculative 'bubble' when prices for it rose dramatically then collapsed, leaving many people penniless.

2. Crops of this plant relied on slave labour in the southern American states.

3. Trade in this plant, along with many other spices, was one of the reasons that Europeans tried to find sea routes to the Far East.

4. During an English civil war the opposing sides chose different colours of this flower.

5. Wreathes made from leaves of this plant were given to ancient Greek athletes and victorious Roman generals.

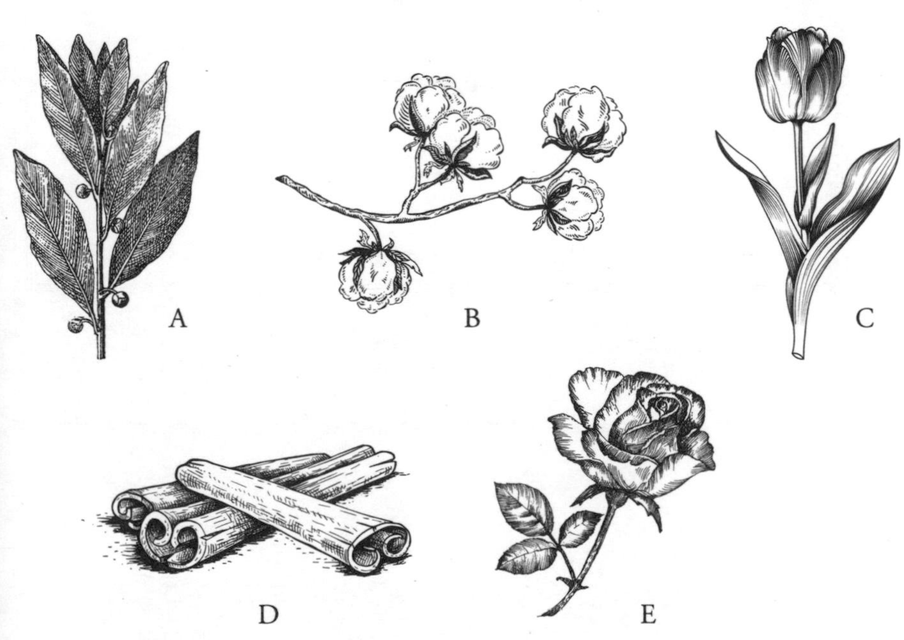

Answers on page 202

Poison in the Bunker

Which of these were not poisoned by senior Nazis in Hitler's bunker as the Russians closed in at the end of the Second World War?

A. Eva Braun's cat Mizzi
B. Hitler's dog Blondi
C. The six children of Nazi propaganda minister Joseph Goebbels

Animal Links

Which is the odd one out of these animals:

Buffalo

Passenger pigeon

Giant kangaroo

Thylacine (Tasmanian tiger)

Great auk

Answers on page 202

Well Travelled

Between AD 789 and 860, who went first to Dorset in southern England, then to Lindisfarne off the Northumbrian coast of England, then to Iona off Scotland, then to Ireland, to Seville in Spain and further afield, including to Constantinople?

Trade Routes

1. Which two civilizations conducted the earliest known long-distance, organized trade?

2. What is the name, reflecting a major commodity, given to the ancient trade routes from southern Arabia to the Mediterranean, and how were goods usually carried along those routes?

3. What name, reflecting another major commodity, is given to the overland trade routes that stretched from China across Central Asia to the Middle East? During the years of Mongol domination of Central Asia, how were these routes affected?

4. In North America, pre-Columbian cultures often used which natural feature on the plains and prairies to facilitate trade movements?

Answers on page 202

North/South Divide

The American Civil War is known by several other names.

1. **Can you come up with at least two alternative names?**
2. **Which states formed the breakaway Confederacy?**
3. **Which states fought for the Union or the 'North'?**
4. **Were there any states that were divided or that sat on the sidelines?**

House of Dread

In 1930, institutions that were hated and feared by poor people finally closed in England and Wales.

What were they?

Answers on pages 202-3

History is Bunk

Who said in 1916 that 'history is more or less bunk'?

Oops, Your Time Machine is Broken

Your time machine has broken down while you are in the year 100 BC, but it will work four more times. There are three events you would really like to visit before you return home but, remember, because of your time machine's quirks you have to visit them in chronological order. In what order do you go to visit:

A. Ada Lovelace creating one of the first ever computer programs for Charles Babbage's Analytical Engine

B. The year that Britain and her allies defeated the French forces under Napoleon Bonaparte at Waterloo

C. The year Cleopatra killed herself in Egypt after her doomed affair with Mark Antony

Answers on page 203

Brazilian Export

In the 1700s a new crop was introduced to Brazil, and by 1900 that country was supplying three-quarters of the world's large demand for the plant's product.

What was the crop?

Partition of Africa

1. What is another name for the colonization of African lands by European countries in the late nineteenth and early twentieth centuries?

2. Where and when did European nations discuss their partition of the continent, and why did they sit down at a conference table to talk about it?

3. How many African nations took part in the conference?

A. 0
B. 1
C. 2

Answers on page 204

Ancient South Asia

Which one of these was not a feature of the Indus Valley cities that thrived from around 2400 BC to 1800 BC:

A. Huge docks
B. Plazas for human sacrifices
C. Granaries
D. Bathing pools

Northern Rebels

When English Saxons in the north of England rebelled against the Norman conquerors in 1069, William the Conqueror (William I of England) responded with a series of vicious reprisals.

What are these known as? How many English males did he have killed in the north?

A. 1 in 10
B. 1 in 5
C. All of them

Answers on page 204

First Journeys

Match these explorers to the routes on the map:

Ferdinand Magellan
Christopher Columbus
Vasco da Gama

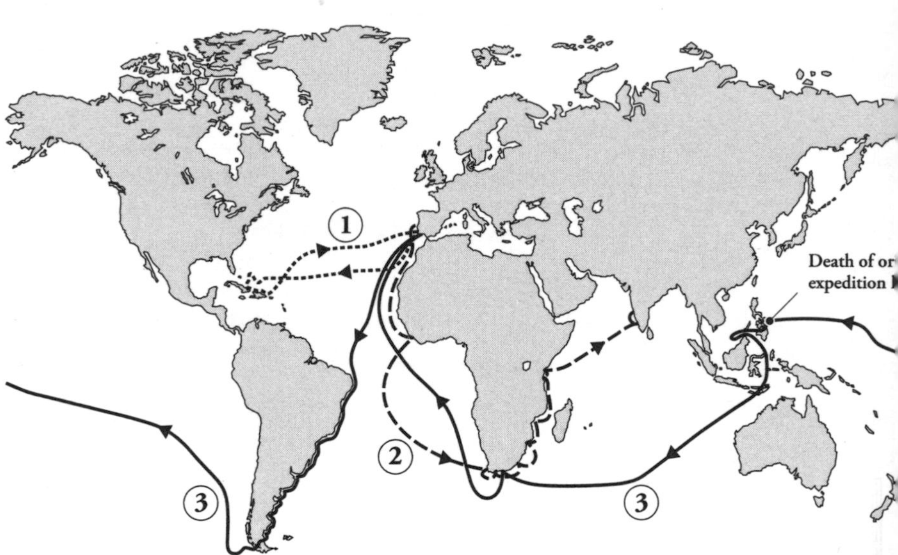

Independence Date

As the Second World War approached its end, what was the first colonized country to declare (and eventually keep) its independence from a European colonial power?

Answers on pages 204-5

Gettysburg Speech

How long was U.S. President Abraham Lincoln's Gettysburg Address in 1863?

A. **1 hour**
B. **2 hours**
C. **2 minutes**

Fill in these gaps:

In the speech Lincoln spoke of the USA as a nation 'conceived in Liberty, and dedicated to the proposition that all men are created ____.' He ended with the words 'government of the people, by the ____, for the____, shall not perish from the ____'.

Irish Rule

What people did Brian Boru defeat in 1002 in order to become king of Ireland?

Answers on page 205

Prehistoric Builders

1. What is the earliest known megalithic (large, prehistoric stones) structure, which is also the world's oldest temple? Approximately when did building start on it?

2. Which extraordinary prehistoric town, in the same country as the first megaliths, contained walls covered with art, including animal remains plastered into the walls?

3. Which Middle-Eastern site was first occupied by hunter-gatherers about 9000 BC but from then on was continuously occupied for thousands of years, growing to become a town, sometimes called a 'proto-city'? It also had some of the earliest known town walls, dating possibly as early as 8000 BC. Clue: There is no archaeological evidence that these walls were blown down in one catastrophic event.

4. Stonehenge in England is a unique stone circle for three reasons to do with the stone structures themselves. Can you name all three?

Anti-Slavery

Which were the last three countries in the Americas to abolish slavery, and when?

Answers on page 205

Military Might

Most of the biggest military occasions known to history were fought in the Second World War.

1. **But before the twentieth century, what is thought to have been the largest invasion force?**

2. **And what was the biggest cavalry charge in history, who led it, and against what army?**

During the Second World War, what was:

3. **The largest ever invasion force?**

4. **The largest ever seaborne invasion force?**

5. **The longest ever siege?**

6. **The fastest ever advance?**

7. **The biggest ever volunteer army?**

8. **The largest and bloodiest ever battle?**

Answers on pages 205-6

Dual Nationalities

What were the original nationalities or affiliations of these rulers?

A. The man who was elected crown prince of Sweden in 1810 and became King Charles XIV John of Sweden and Norway in 1818. His descendants still rule Sweden.

B. Catherine the Great of Russia

C. Marie Antoinette of France

D. William III of England

E. Kublai Khan of China

New Jobs for Old

In 1851 65,000 people in Britain were working in jobs that hadn't existed thirty years earlier, all in what we would nowadays describe as one 'sector'.

What was it?

A. Railways
B. Canals
C. Iron foundries

Answers on page 206

Women Warriors

Which of these were not historically attested women warriors?

A. An eighteenth- to nineteenth-century royal regiment in Dahomey, West Africa (now Benin)

B. The Mayan princess Itzel-Kuk who led the successful defence of her city in the ninth-century Mayan civil wars

C. The 'Night Witches', the Russian all-female bomber pilots during the Second World War

D. General Fu Hao of Shang dynasty China, the world's first known female war leader

E. Queen Artemesia I of Halicarnassus, who led several ships to take part in the Persian invasion of Greece in 480 BC

Answer on page 206

World Firsts

1. What is considered to be the world's first civilization, which built the first cities and developed the first writing in the world?

2. As a bonus point, what name did these people give to their lands, and what does that name mean?

3. Where was it situated?

4. How was this civilization organized?

   A. One mega-city dominating the region
   B. City-states
   C. A travelling court ruled by elected governors

5. The region also saw the world's first empire. Can you name that empire, explain why it was called that, and name the first empire-builder?

Answers on page 206

Population Pressure

Which empire was the largest in terms of the percentage of the world's population it contained?

Answer on page 207

Common Ground

What do these places have in common?

Promontory Point, Utah, USA in 1869

Paris and Constantinople in 1883

Craigellachie, British Columbia, Canada in 1885

Moscow and Vladivostok, Russia in 1905

Perth and Sydney, Australia in 1917

Angola and Tanzania or Mozambique in 1929

A Much-Travelled Group

Which organization travelled from Jerusalem to Rhodes, then from Rhodes to Malta, then to Saint Petersburg in Russia, then to Rome, and finally, in different forms, to many countries around the world?

Answers on page 207

True or False?

The people who first populated Australia arrived from South America.

What Decade is This?

George Washington is inaugurated as the first president of the USA

The French Revolution begins

Immanuel Kant writes *Critique of Pure Reason*, one of the foundational works of modern philosophy

Wolfgang Amadeus Mozart is composing

The Montgolfier brothers ascend in a hot-air balloon

Brighton Pavilion is built in England

A settlement for freed slaves is founded in Sierra Leone

Luigi Aloisio Galvani is exploring the electric function of dead frogs' muscles

Answers on page 207

Mass Deaths

What killed at least a third of the population of Europe between 1347 and 1351?

Answer on page 207

Freedom Fighters

In the Latin American Wars of Independence, which group of people were the main instigators of the rebellions against Spanish rule?

A. Native Americans
B. Enslaved Africans
C. Mestizos, people of mixed Spanish and indigenous race
D. Ruling aristocrats of Spanish descent

Aviation Milestone

What did Chuck Yeager break in his Bell X-1 plane in 1947?

Answers on page 208

Five, Four, Three, Two, One

5 FIRSTS

1. When was the First Reich and who founded it? What was it also known as?

2. Who had the Terracotta Army built?

3. Who was the inventor who demonstrated the first true television system in 1926?

4. What name was given to Britain's first colony in Australia?

5. Who carried out the first sustained, powered, manned flight?

4 SECONDS

1. Who was the second U.S. president?

2. What nationality were the second European people to forge a settlement in what is now Canada?

3. When was the Second Reich and who founded it? What was it also known as?

4. In what century was the Second French Republic founded?

3 THIRDS

1. When was the Third Reich and who founded it? What is it commonly known as?

2. In 1403 the third emperor of the Ming Dynasty in China, the Yongle Emperor, moved his capital from Nanjing, the southern capital, to a new northern capital. What city is that today?

3. Who was the third original member, with Britain and France, of the Allied or Entente powers during the First World War?

2 FOURTHS

1. Who was the fourth crowned Tudor monarch of England and Wales?

2. Sejong the Great was the fourth monarch of the Joseon dynasty and presided over a Golden Age. What country did he rule?

1 FIFTH

1. In 1791 the Bill of Rights was ratified in the USA, including the Fifth Amendment to the U.S. Constitution. Which part of this amendment is commonly known as 'pleading the Fifth'?

Answers on page 208

Snakes and Ladders

Answer the questions to climb the ladders and win the game. If you get the answers wrong, you may end up sliding down a snake back to the beginning.

1. Subtract the number of world wars from the number of wives that King Henry VIII of England married.

2. The number of years of the eighteenth-century war that is also known as the French and Indian War.

3. Ivan the Terrible was the first tsar of all Russia. But what number did he carry as Ivan, Prince of Muscovy?

4. How many ships sailed with Christopher Columbus when he first crossed the Atlantic to reach the Americas?

5. What year did the First World War end? Subtract from that date the name of a very long-running war between England and France that saw the Battle of Crecy among other conflicts. Now subtract the number of years of a shorter, but still long-running conflict in central Europe that began in 1618. Finally, how many years from this date did the French Revolution begin?

6. How many husbands did Mary Queen of Scots have?

Answers on page 209

64	63	62	61	60	59	58	57
49	50	51	52	53	54	55	56
48	47	46	45	44	43	42	41
33	34	35	36	37	38	39	40
32	31	30	29	28	27	26	25
17	18	19	20	21	22	23	24
16	15	14	13	12	11	10	9
1	2	3	4	5	6	7	8

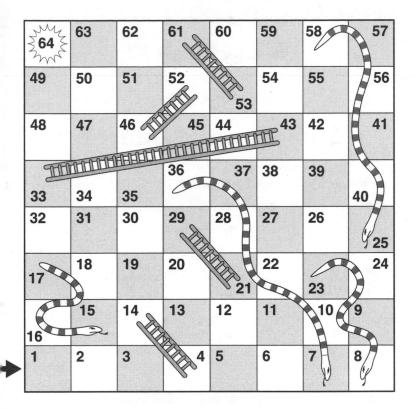

Shooting Gallery?

True or false?

In 1889 an American sharpshooter travelling in Europe with Buffalo Bill Cody's Wild West Show performed the trick of shooting the ash off a cigarette held by a man, without harming the holder, on German Kaiser Wilhelm II. When the First World War began, the sharpshooter wrote to the Kaiser asking for another shot.

Who was the sharpshooter this story is told about?

Answers on page 209

What Links?

What do the following people have in common?

Hammurabi of Babylon
Eastern Roman Emperor Justinian I
Charlemagne
King John of England
Napoleon Bonaparte

Answer on pages 209-10

Mughal India

The Mughal Empire was India's biggest empire since ancient days.

1. Who founded it, and which great warlords was he descended from?

2. Which emperor saw the Mughal Empire reach its greatest extent in South Asia and become the world's biggest economy at the time?

3. The empire began to fragment soon after his death in 1707, but which power eventually brought an official end to the Mughal Empire?

Answers on page 210

Chinese Revolution

Who was the primary mover in the 1911 revolution that overthrew thousands of years of Imperial rule in China?

A. Chiang Kai-shek
B. Sun Yat-sen
C. Mao Zedong

Votes for Women

1. Can you list the first five countries to give all women the vote in national elections? Even more impressively, can you give the years that suffrage was granted?

2. What were the first two countries to formally allow women to stand for parliamentary election, and when?

Answers on page 210

Plain Dealing

The nomads who roamed the Eurasian steppes often had a major impact on the settled societies around the plains.

1. Which people were known for small gold ornaments often featuring stylized, expressive animal motifs?

2. What barrier was built in the East to keep the nomads out?

3. Which people inflicted a crushing defeat on the Romans at Carrhae and were known for shooting arrows while turning in the saddle to face backwards?

4. Which people forged the largest contiguous land empire in history?

5. What technological innovations were developed on the steppes?

Horrible Deaths

True or false?

More soldiers in the First World War died from infection rather than from battlefield injuries.

Answers on page 210

Victoria's Children

This is a simplified family tree of Queen Victoria of Britain.

Fill in the boxes marked with a dash. Please give as much detail as you can about the titles of the missing people, as well as their first or most commonly used name. (*Don't overlook the dash next to William on the second row.*)

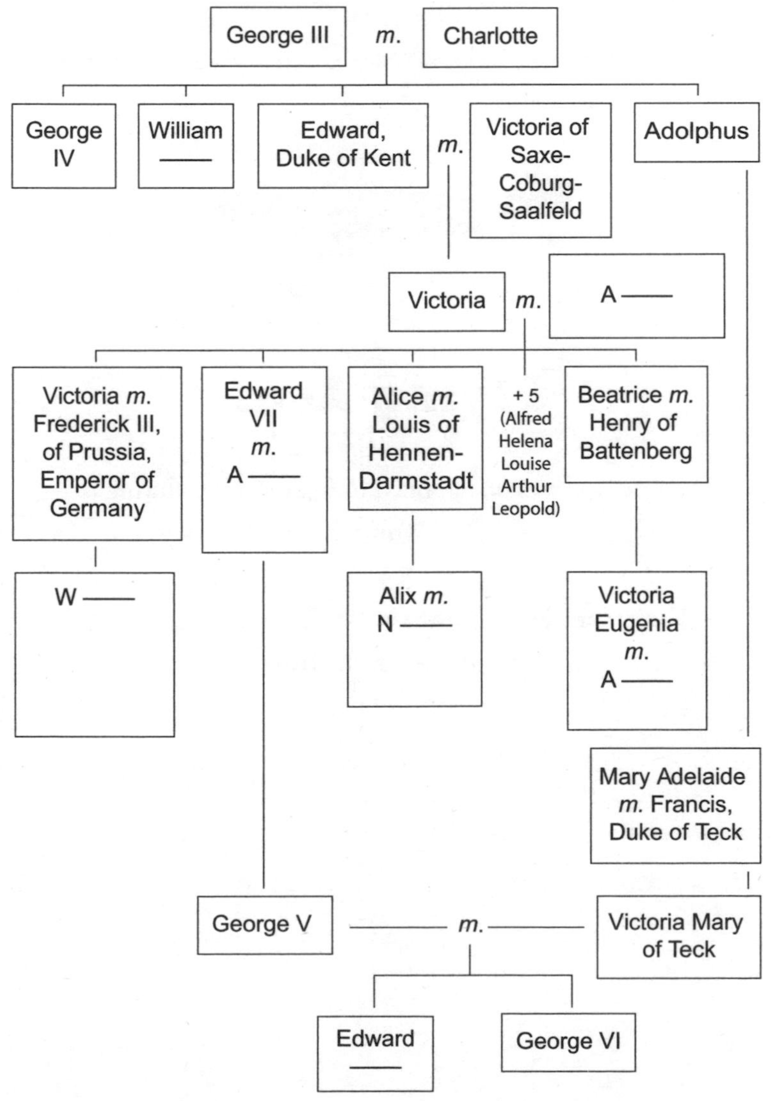

Answers on page 211

Oldest Rulers

Which country claims to have the world's longest continuous hereditary monarchy, and back to what date does it trace its line?

Flying Aces

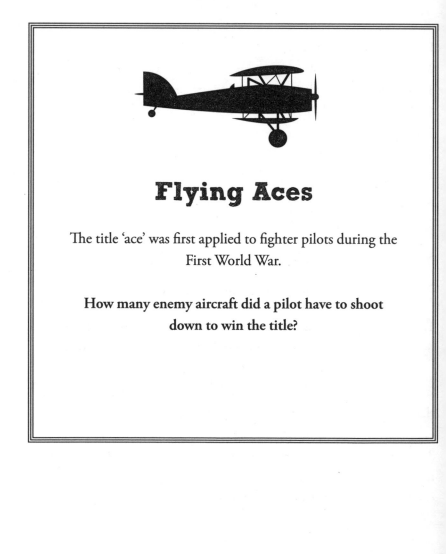

The title 'ace' was first applied to fighter pilots during the First World War.

How many enemy aircraft did a pilot have to shoot down to win the title?

Answers on page 212

Do You Know Your Ancestors?

In which countries were these important archaeological discoveries made, which provided evidence of early human ancestors or of early human settlement?

1. The Laetoli footprints
2. Denisova cave, home of the Denisovan hominin species
3. Neander Valley, after which Neanderthals were named
4. The small hominins known as 'hobbits'
5. Sterkfontein caves
6. Choukoutien caves
7. Clovis point stone tools (major centres)

Baltic Trade

1. What was the name of the trading and defensive network set up by German towns and mercantile interests in the twelfth century?

2. What was one of the major commodities its members traded that was essential for shipbuilding?

3. The network grew to encompass nearly 200 members across northern Europe. Can you name all 200 of them? Only joking – can you name just the network's central city?

Answers on page 212

Universal Declaration

In 1948, the members of an international organization signed a Universal Declaration of Human Rights.

What was this organization, which was founded after the Second World War to maintain international peace and security?

Interrupted

What began in 776 BC, ended in AD 393, but was resumed in 1896?

A Merger

What single colony, later a country of the same name, was formed by the merger of Italy's three North African colonies in 1934?

Answers on page 212

The Tale of Nefertari

Fill in the gaps in this story:

Nefertari was a noblewoman in ancient Egypt, who married the pharaoh Ramesses II, also known as Ramesses the ____ . He ruled in the XIX dynasty, which was founded by Ramesses ____ in 1292 BC. Nefertari's husband was called ____ in later Greek histories, and thousands of years later Percy Bysshe Shelley wrote a poem with that name as its title. Nefertari and Ramesses built an enormous temple at Abu Simbel, with colossal statues of themselves. Ramesses was a warlike pharaoh, and his Battle of ____ against the Hittites was the first battle in history about which we have records of the tactics and strategy. Ramesses achieved another world first, when he wrote a ____ with the Hittites following the battle, the first in recorded history. The Hittites forged a Middle Eastern empire from their base in the present-day country of ____ . Nefertari was Ramesses' most important wife, and he said of her that she was the one 'for whom the ____ shines'. She was highly intelligent, and learned the difficult skill of reading the Egyptian picture language, ____ . This helped her in the diplomatic role she adopted, writing letters of friendship to the Hittite ____ , which helped maintain peace between the two peoples. When Nefertari died around 1255 BC, Ramesses buried her in a magnificent tomb in the Valley of the ____ . The art in her tomb provides important information about the ancient Egyptians' beliefs about ____ .

Answers on pages 212-13

Revolutionary Times

What country saw an October Manifesto, a February Revolution, an October Revolution and a Five-Year Plan?

Human Rights

What is widely considered to be the first charter of human rights?

Who wrote it, what were its general principles, and how did he or she put their principles into action in a famous historical city and for an exiled people?

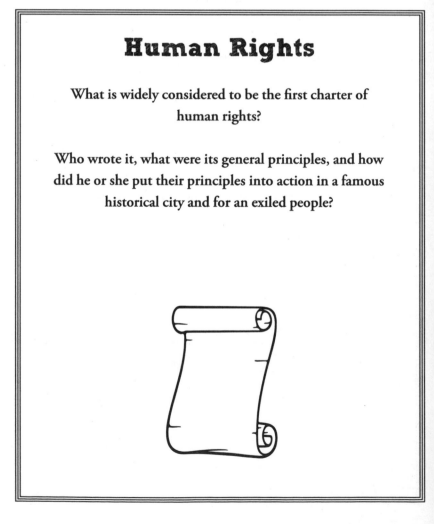

Answers on page 213

Cultural Works

Match these artistic, literary or musical people to their cultural movement or work:

Christina Rossetti	*Swan Lake*	painting
Pablo Picasso	*The Age of Bronze*	poetry
Pyotr Ilyich Tchaikovsky	*All Quiet on the Western Front*	sculpture
Erich Maria Remarque	*Goblin Market*	ballet
François-Auguste-René Rodin	Rose Period	literature

Olympic Bubble

Where were the 1936 Olympic Games held?

Who punctured Hitler's hope that his German 'Aryans' would dominate the games?

And how many medals did this athlete win?

Answers on page 213

Attack Plan

Which people fought in this formation, and what was it known as?

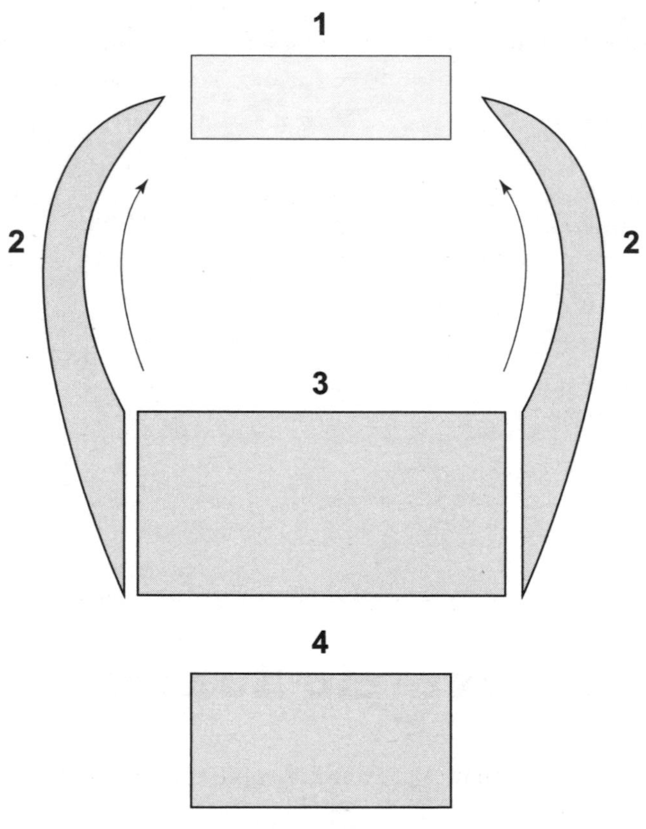

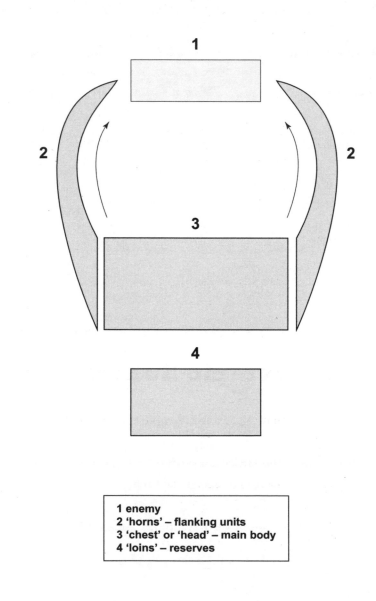

1 enemy
2 'horns' – flanking units
3 'chest' or 'head' – main body
4 'loins' – reserves

Answers on page 214

Roman Soldiers

By about AD 100 the Roman army had settled into its final structure.

1. **From then on, how many men did a centurion command?**

2. **What was the original number that a centurion commanded?**

3. **What was the name given to a Roman army?**

4. **A Roman army was formed from cohorts and centuries. Which was the smaller unit, and how many of them went into the larger unit?**

5. **How many of the larger units formed the army?**

6. **These men were infantry, but what other type of soldiers accompanied a Roman army?**

Dynamic Awards

Which international awards were first given in 1901?

The man who founded the awards made a great deal of his money from two explosive inventions.

What were they?

Answers on page 214

Odd Culture

Which one of these cultural movements is the odd one out?

Modernism
Impressionism
Cubism
Surrealism

Empire State

What empire of 327 BC is marked here?

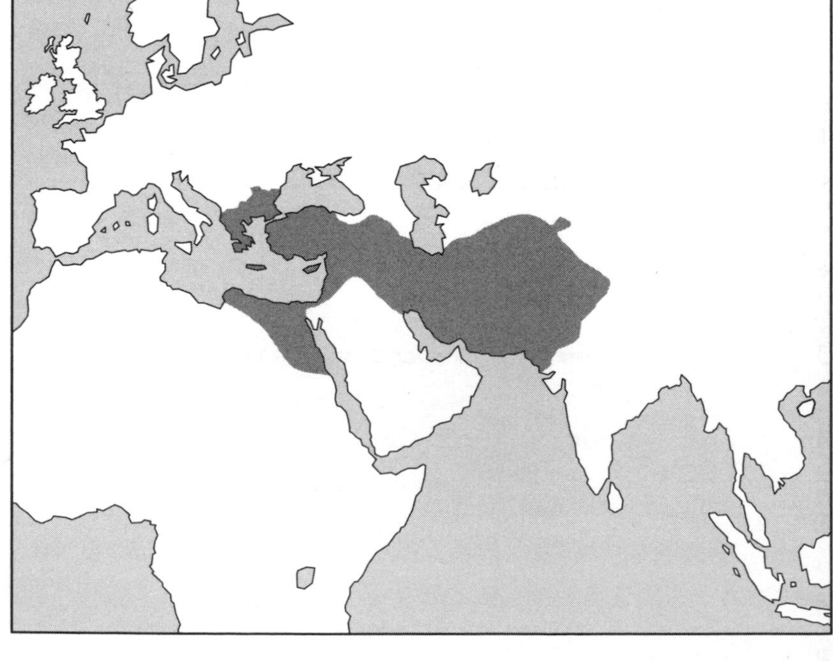

Answers on page 214

Plays Well With Others

In 1540 King Henry VIII of England banned a popular sport because too many men were becoming injured from playing it.

Which was it?

A. Football
B. Rugby
C. Cricket

Old Cities, New Cities

1. What was the city of New Amsterdam renamed as in 1664?

2. In 1793 Peter the Great of Russia founded a new capital city. During the First World War the Russians patriotically changed the German elements in its name to Russian elements. What was it first called and what was it changed to? Then, during the Communist era, it was given which new name?

3. Edo is the old name for which Asian capital city?

4. Dunedin is the old name for a Scottish city. The old name probably refers to a hill fort whose site is still a major stronghold. What city is this?

5. The Aztec city of Tenochtitlan is now within the bounds of which modern city?

Answers on page 214

Lasting Conflict

Which international conflict began almost immediately after the Second World War ended in 1945?

Answer on page 214

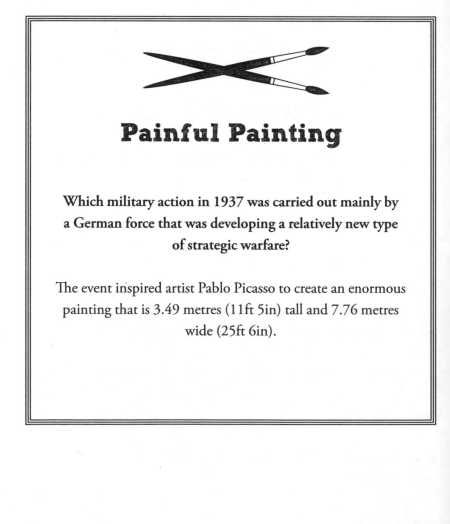

Painful Painting

Which military action in 1937 was carried out mainly by a German force that was developing a relatively new type of strategic warfare?

The event inspired artist Pablo Picasso to create an enormous painting that is 3.49 metres (11ft 5in) tall and 7.76 metres wide (25ft 6in).

Answers on page 215

Musical First

What musical instrument was first produced by Adolph Rickenbacher (Rickenbacker) in 1932 and went on to become a hugely influential part of popular music?

A. Theremin
B. Saxophone
C. Electric guitar

No Gold Medal

Which one of these sports was not once part of the modern Olympics?

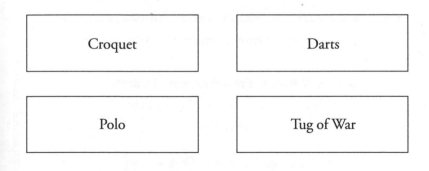

Croquet	Darts
Polo	Tug of War

Answers on page 215

Arts and Crafts Timeline

Put these works of art, buildings or craft movements in chronological order:

1. Claude Monet's *Water Lilies* series
2. The heyday of trench art
3. *American Gothic* by Grant Wood
4. *The Garden of Earthly Delights* by Hieronymus Bosch
5. *The Great Wave* by Hokusai
6. Michelangelo's statue of David
7. *The Night Watch*, by Rembrandt van Rijn
8. The city of Great Zimbabwe
9. Lascaux cave paintings, France
10. *Whistler's Mother* by James MacNeill Whistler

Independence Now

Which country saw a twentieth-century independence movement known as the Non-Cooperation Movement?

Who was the movement's leader?

Riotous Ballet

Which innovative Russian ballet caused an uproar, sometimes described as a riot, when it was first performed in Paris in 1913?

Answers on page 215

Giant Encounter

Once thought by Westerners to be a mythical animal, which large Asian creature was first seen as a live specimen by a European in 1916?

A. Giant panda
B. Yeti
C. Indonesian elephant

Answer on page 215

The Terrible Trenches

This map shows the location of five important battles that took place on the Western Front in the First World War.

Can you identify each battle, and for an impressive virtual bonus point, can you put them in date order?

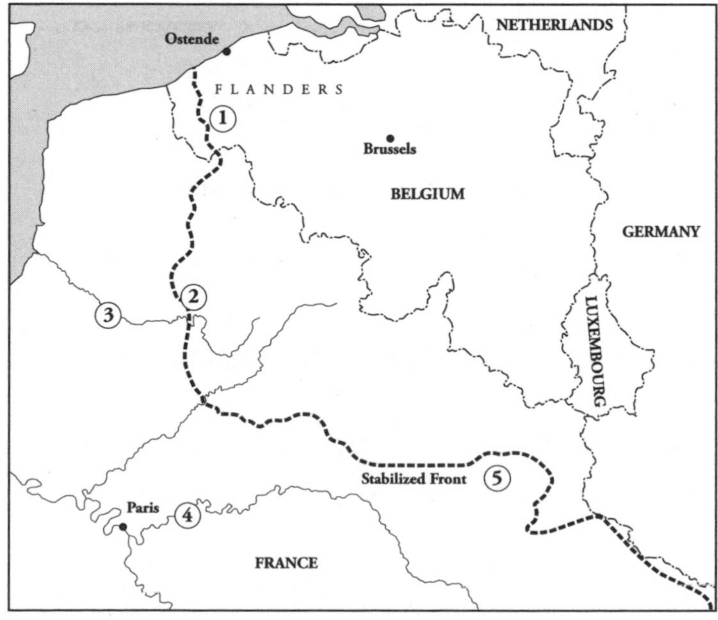

Answers on page 216

European Recovery

What was the name of the American scheme that began in 1948 to give aid to war-torn European countries?

A. The Truman Doctrine
B. The Marshall Plan
C. The Monroe Plan

Answer on page 216

Music to Grow Up With

In 1936 a symphony written specifically for children was first performed in Moscow, Russia. The characters in the story are represented by different musical instruments, and it has become one of the most widely performed pieces of classical music.

What is the symphony and who composed it?

House of Wisdom

In what city was the House of Wisdom, the most important centre of learning in the eighth and ninth centuries?

Answers on page 217

Building the Past

Build up a picture of the past by finding the match between the names, places, architectural styles, buildings, features, or works in the first column with their correct counterparts in the second column.

Done that? Great. Now put them in chronological order.

Le Corbusier	King Ludwig II's fairy-tale castles
Chicago	Golden Temple
Vitruvius	Bauhaus
Walter Gropius	*On Architecture*
Crystal Palace	First skyscraper
Bavaria	Romanesque/Gothic
Acropolis	Great Ziggurat
Chrysler Building	Renaissance
Amritsar	New industrial materials, e.g. cast iron
Filippo Brunelleschi	Art deco
Mont-Saint-Michel	Temple to Athena
Ur	Villa Savoye

Answers on page 217

A Matter of Gravity

Between 1589 and 1592 the scientist Galileo reportedly experimented with mass and gravity by dropping different materials from the top of a tall building.

What building was it?

Odd One Out

Which one of these British battles is the odd one out?

Dunbar	Edgehill
Inverkeithing	Torrington
Towton	

Answers on page 217

Whose Family is This?

This is a simplified family tree of a very convoluted and somewhat inbred ruling European family from around 1415 to around 1864.

What is the family and, because of the inbreeding, what physical characteristic did several members of the family possess?

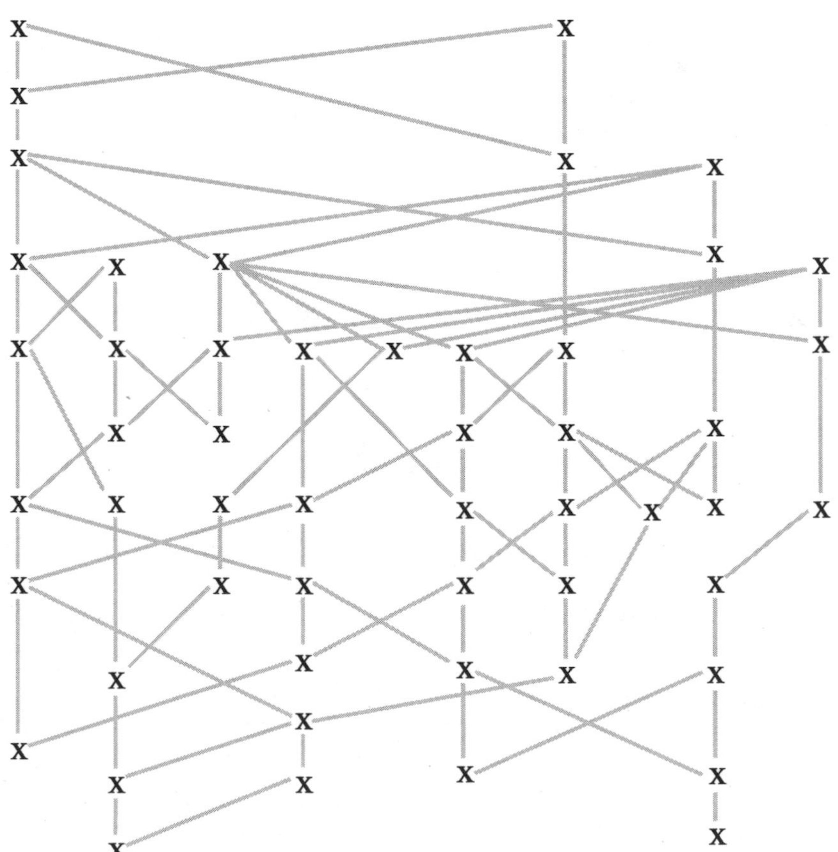

Answers on page 218

Medical Breakthroughs

Can you match these medical advances with the person who discovered or promoted them, then put them in their chronological order?

Aspirin	Marie Curie	1860s
Iron lung	Wilhelm Röntgen	1857
Epidemiology / method of cholera infection	Joseph Lister	From 1949
Psychoanalytic theory	Felix Hoffmann	1895
Germ theory of disease	Karl Landsteiner	1901
Anaesthetics	William Morton	1902
Discovery of radium	Jane C. Wright	1846
X-rays	Sigmund Freud	1854
Chemotherapy	John Snow	1927
Blood groups / safe blood transfusions	Edward Jenner	1899
Disinfectants	Philip Drinker	1796
Breakthrough in smallpox inoculation	Louis Pasteur	1895

Answers on page 218

The Red Flag

The flag of the Communist USSR featured a hammer and sickle.

What did these symbolize?

Oil!

In 1908 a major oil field was discovered that kick-started the oil industry in that area.

Was it in Iran, Texas or Saudi Arabia?

Answers on page 219

Odd Musical Style

Which of these musical styles is the odd one out?

Blues	Calypso
Jazz	Bluegrass

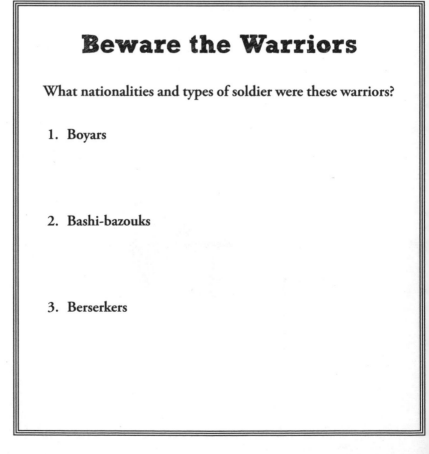

Beware the Warriors

What nationalities and types of soldier were these warriors?

1. Boyars

2. Bashi-bazouks

3. Berserkers

Answers on page 219

Oldest Parliament

Which is the world's oldest parliament?

A. The Althing of Iceland
B. The Diet of Germany
C. The Parliament of Great Britain

Heartfelt Quote

Who said,

'I know I have the body but of a weak and feeble woman; but I have the heart and stomach of a king . . .'

and on what occasion?

Debut Appearance

Who made his first public appearance in the film *Steamboat Willie* in 1928?

Answers on page 219

Help the Historian

Find the paths that will help the historian reach the historic books.

The other path leads to a historian's worst nightmare – an empty bookcase.

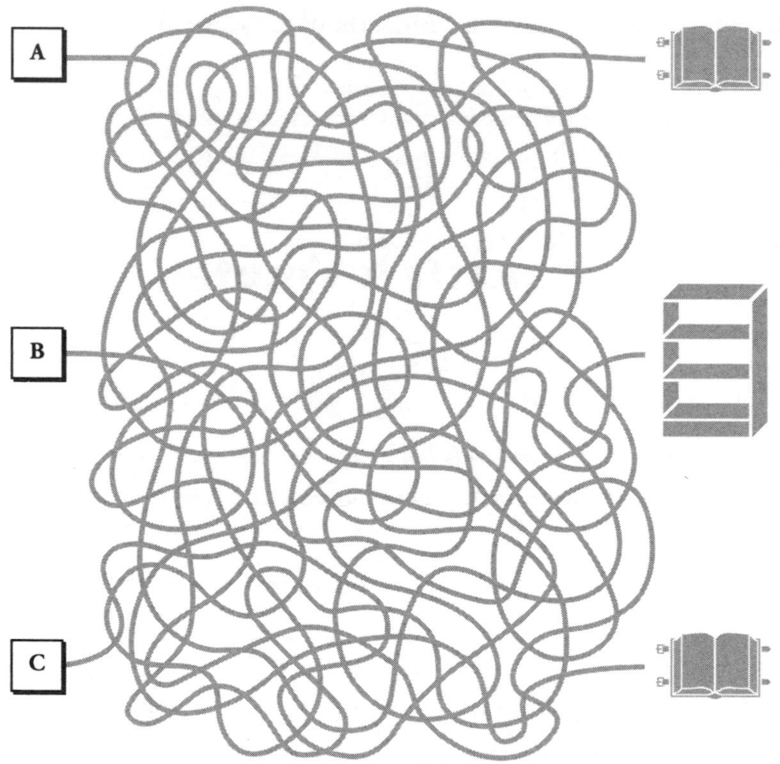

Deadly Weapon

Which weapon was instrumental in the English victory at the Battle of Agincourt in 1415?

Answers on page 220

Capital Choice

Why did Philip II of Spain choose Madrid to be the first national capital city of Spain in 1561?

A. It had an important river running through it giving easy transport links to the rest of the country and to the coast

B. It had a large population and already had a major palace

C. He did not want to offend any of the larger Spanish cities by choosing one of them over the others, so he picked Madrid since it was then a smallish, insignificant town

One Year, Many Events

These events all took place in the same year. But what century was it?

Tokugawa Ieyasu won the Battle of Sekigahara in Japan and began the Tokugawa Shogunate

El Greco painted *Christ Driving the Money Changers from the Temple*

During the Dutch War of Independence, the Dutch won a tactical battle over the Spanish at Nieuwpoort

The Italian philosopher and scientist Giordano Bruno was burnt at the stake for heresy

William Shakespeare's plays *A Midsummer Night's Dream* and *The Merchant of Venice* were published

Answers on page 220

Sailing Through History

Can you match these fleets to their purpose?

1. **India Armadas**
2. **The First Fleet**
3. **The Triangular Trade and the Middle Passage**
4. **Silver Fleets**
5. **Sea Beggars**
6. **Ming Treasure Fleets**
7. **Sea Peoples**
8. **The Great Tea Race**

The three-leg Atlantic slave trade between the late sixteenth and early nineteenth centuries. First, European ships took mainly manufactured trade goods to Africa; then, on the middle journey, enslaved Africans were transported to the American colonies or to the Caribbean. The ships then carried primarily raw materials back to Europe.

Maritime raiders who terrorized the south-east Mediterranean coastlines from around 1276 BC. Ramesses III of Egypt destroyed them in 1178 BC.

The fleet carrying the British convicts, settlers, marines, etc. who founded the first colony in Australia. Leaving England on 13 May 1787, it arrived in Botany Bay on 15 January 1788.

A competition between the clippers bringing tea from China to Britain in the nineteenth century. The rivalry to be the first ship to arrive with the new season's crop culminated in a prize race conducted in 1866.

Answers on pages 220-1

Trade fleets from Portugal to Asia and back from 1497 to 1511.

The Dutch rebel navy who fought against Spanish rule from the late sixteenth century.

Also called the West Indies Fleets, they were the convoys bringing goods and treasure to Spain from its lands in the Americas from 1566 to 1790.

Seven huge exploratory expeditions launched by the Chinese Yongle Emperor. They were led by Admiral Zheng He between 1405 and 1433. Carrying treasure as gifts, they expanded Chinese influence and authority as well as knowledge of the world.

Young Turks

What did the Young Turks of the early nineteenth century protest about in Turkey?

A. The high age requirement for attending university
B. The lack of a constitution
C. The lack of modern art schools

Answer on page 221

Odd One Out

Which of these ancient battles is the odd one out? Why?

Tanagra

Marathon

Thermopylae

Salamis

Social Reforms

William Gladstone, British prime minister for four terms between 1868 and 1894, introduced several social reforms in Britain.

Which of these was not included?

A. **Free education for all children**
B. **Working hours were reduced to eight hours a day**
C. **A secret ballot in elections**
D. **Promotion in the army would be by merit, not social rank**

Answers on page 221

Whose Republic?

In what country was the Weimar Republic from 1919 to 1933?

Odd Philosophy Out

All except one of these philosophical movements developed in the early twentieth century.

Which is the odd one out?

Logical positivism

Existentialism

Metaphysics

Phenomenology

Analytic philosophy

Answers on page 221

What's the Link?

What do these states have in common?

The Ashanti Empire

Bohemia

Burgundy

Grenada

Tibet

Oldest Trophy

With which sports are these trophies associated, and which of them is the oldest international sporting trophy?

A. America's Cup
B. Jules Rimet Trophy
C. Stanley Cup

Answers on page 222

A Good Year

What did Charles Goodyear perfect in 1839, making a breakthrough while he was in prison for debt?

A. Tyres
B. Vulcanized rubber
C. Blimps

A Saving Plan

What was first introduced in some parts of Canada in 1908, then was adopted by Germany and Austria to save fuel during the First World War?

Many other countries then swiftly copied them.

Typeset

Who produced the first metal movable-type printing press in Europe?

Answers on page 222

What Were They?

What category of object did all these obsolete European things belong to, and what were they individually?

1. **Chiton**
2. **Liripipe**
3. **Banyan**
4. **Polonaise**
5. **Stola**
6. **Chopines**

A Busy Decade

The first edition of the *Encyclopaedia Britannica* was completed in the same decade that Richard Arkwright built his first spinning mill in England, the La Scala Opera House was opened in Milan, Italy, and the world's first educational institution devoted solely to teaching engineering was founded in Istanbul.

What decade was it?

A. **1740s**
B. **1770s**
C. **1820s**

Answers on pages 222-3

49ers

Who were the 'Forty-niners' in nineteenth-century USA?

A French Sequence

What does this sequence show?

French King Louis XVI

French Queen Marie Antoinette

Scientist Antoine Lavoisier

Politician Maximilien Robespierre

Answers on page 223

Code Names

In 1945, who were Little Boy and Fat Man?

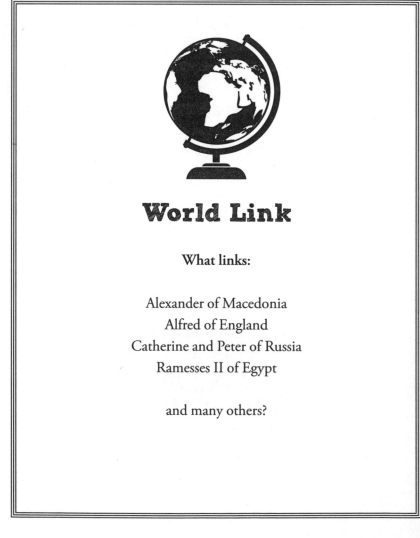

World Link

What links:

Alexander of Macedonia
Alfred of England
Catherine and Peter of Russia
Ramesses II of Egypt

and many others?

Answers on page 223

State of the Union

Which independent republic, formerly a province of Mexico, was annexed by the United States in 1845?

Who Lived Here?

Before the American Civil War, who lived at Arlington House on the Potomac River?

During the war, this mansion and its extensive grounds were very early on taken over by the Union as a hospital and cemetery, becoming Arlington National Cemetery.

Renamed

What name did the Kingdom of the Hejaz and Nejd take in 1932?

Answers on page 223

FEELING CONFIDENT?

LET'S SEE HOW WELL YOU'VE DONE ...

NICKNAMES

A. The Lionheart
B. The She-Wolf
C. The Desert Fox
D. The Iron Chancellor
E. The Sun King
F. The Liberator
G. The Riveter

ENGINELESS

Clément Ader (an early aviator)

LAUGHING AT THE PAST

1. The American Civil War
2. The Second World War
3. The American Wild West in 1874
4. Medieval France
5. *Carry On Up the Khyber*

DYNASTIC DUO

Isabella I of Castile and Ferdinand II of Aragon

WORTHLESS

A. Bananas

Playing cards were used as money in a few countries, particularly during the seventeenth century in the French colonies that became part of Canada. Salt bars or cakes were used as currency in parts of Asia and many parts of Africa. Shell money was known in Africa, the Americas, Asia and Australia.

HIDDEN TREASURES

There are twenty-one objects. The European-style **crown** is the anachronistic odd one out.

FOOD FACTS AND FABLES

1. **False.** Kedgeree developed from the centuries-old Indian dish *khichiri*, which was adapted for British tastes to create the modern dish.

2. **True.** The first dry packaged mix, for custard, was launched in the 1840s in Britain.
3. **False.** Hamburgers are named after the German city of Hamburg, where a similar meat patty was eaten.
4. **False.** It was during the Second World War that many American servicemen encountered pizzas in Southern Italy and wanted to eat them again on their return to the USA.
5. **True.** The Earl of Sandwich (or, rather, his cook) may not have invented modern sandwiches, but they became popular after his legendary game of cards as people demanded convenience food the 'same as Sandwich'.
6. **False.** Fortune cookies were invented in California in the 1930s as a marketing ploy to attract diners to a Chinese restaurant.
7. **True.** At this point Napoleon was a long way away from food supplies, so it is thought that his steward assembled the ingredients that were available to form a new recipe.
8. **True.** Lead was used in the solder to seal a tin and could contaminate the food.
9. **False.** Cocaine was, indeed, one of Coke's original ingredients, but it was removed from the drink in about 1903.
10. **False**. Paella was developed over time in Valencia, Spain.

ISLAND BAN

The hula dance

IMPORTANT ELEVENS

It was the time and date of the armistice that ended hostilities in the First World War: the eleventh hour of the eleventh day in the eleventh month, i.e. 11 o'clock in the morning of 11th November.

ROMAN MINI CROSSWORD

1. Livia (Livia Drusilla)
2. Venus
3. Pompeii
4. *across* Cannae
4. *down* Cicero
5. Marcus (Mark Antony)
6. Remus
7. Julius or Iulius (Julius Caesar)

The anagram is Via Appia.

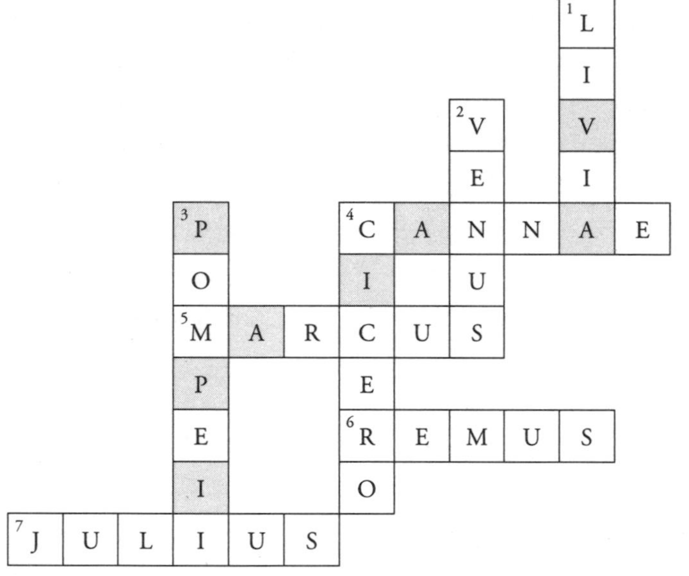

FILM NIGHT, PART 1

1. Mayan city states
2. *Seven Samurai*
3. Taking indigenous children from their families and bringing them up in residential schools
4. The Battle of Rorke's Drift
5. Atlanta, in the south
6. King of the Arab Kingdom of Syria, then King of Iraq

A ROMANTIC SPORT?

B. Baseball

THE TALE OF TROY

Homer
Ilion
Euripides
Menelaus
Paris
Troy
Ten
Horse
Alexander the Great
Schliemann
Turkey
Agamemnon

FOOTSTEPS PICTOGRAM

This portrays the Long March from October 1934 to October 1935, when Chinese communist forces retreated from the nationalists during the Chinese Civil War.

A COMMON TOUCH, PART 1

They all had red hair

PREHISTORIC HAIRSTYLES AND HATS

1. Mohawk or mohican, a hairstyle that has the sides of the head shaved but the middle of the hair is grown long to stick upwards, and is often held upright only by the use of cosmetics, which it seems Clonycavan Man did use.
2. A) Sheepskin/wool
3. I) The Copper Age, part of the Late Neolithic
   II) C) Tattoos
   III) B) Bearskin
4. A chinstrap
5. They were all killed. Clonycavan Man and Tollund Man may have been ritual sacrifices, and Ötzi may have died from blood loss after an arrow wound.

SCIENTIFIC TIME TRAVEL

C. In AD 499 **Aryabhata** wrote an important book on mathematics which explored the concept of zero, although he probably did not invent the mathematical use of zero.

B. **Isaac Newton** worked out his famous laws in 1666, partly inspired by seeing an apple fall from a tree, but it did not hit him on the head.

A. **Alexander Graham Bell** made the first telephone call in 1876.

E. **Marie Curie** was appointed the first female professor at the University of Paris in 1906. She coined the term 'radioactivity'.

D. **Alexander Fleming** discovered penicillin, the first antibiotic, in 1928 when he observed that mould that grew on a bacteria sample had killed some of the bacteria.

NAME THE HISTORIAN

Thucydides *c.* 431 BC, *The History of the Peloponnesian War*
Ban Zhao AD 111, *Book of Han*
Bede *c.* AD 731, *The Ecclesiastical History of the English People*
Jean Froissart *c.* 1369, *Chronicles*

WINDOW ON THE PAST

The Defenestration of Prague, when political disagreements led to people being thrown out of windows.

PEACE TREATY

The Palace of Versailles in France. The agreement became known as the Treaty of Versailles.

COLOURFUL SOLDIERS

Red Army: Communist forces who won the Russian Civil War and became the army of the USSR

Redshirts: Garibaldi's soliders during the nineteenth-century campaigns that led to Italian unification

Redcoats: British soldiers from the seventeenth century to the twentieth century, although some units of the British army still wear red tunics

Brownshirts: The *Sturmabteilung* (Storm Troopers) or SA, a paramilitary force that helped Hitler rise to power in Nazi Germany

Blackshirts: Mussolini's fascist militia in 1920s Italy; blackshirts was also the name given to British fascists in the 1930s

Golden Horde: A Mongol khanate that ruled much of Eastern Europe and the Caucasus from the 1240s until 1502

William of Orange (William I, Prince of Orange): Leading figure in the Dutch War of Independence against Habsburg Spain

White Guard: Anti-communist soldiers in the Russian Civil War of 1917–1922/23

FIRST WORLD WAR CAMPAIGN

The Gallipoli Campaign, sometimes known as the Dardanelles Campaign.

A RELUCTANT ROAD

The Native Americans were forced to move to so-called 'Indian Territory'. The collective name for their journeys is 'Trail of Tears', from a description of the removal of Cherokee people.

OTTOMAN GLORY

The Magnificent

A NAVAL CLASH

A. The Battle of Midway between the USA and Japan

1. The Battle of Midway was a victory for the United States and is considered to be one of the 'turning points' of the Second World War, since Japan lost its four fleet aircraft carriers along with other ships, nearly 300 aircraft and thousands of experienced men. From then on Japan was not able to continue to expand its perimeter in the Pacific.

2. Only a few members of the Japanese high command were told the truth about the battle. Japanese news presented it as a victory. Apart from the senior officers, wounded Japanese men were kept in quarantine and fit men were immediately sent to units in the South Pacific so that word of the defeat could not spread at home.

3. Before the battle American cryptographers had managed to break a Japanese code so the U.S. Navy was able to prepare for what the Japanese had intended to be a surprise attack on their bases on Midway Island.

FIRST WORLD WAR MAZE

This is the safe route for the soldier (see opposite).

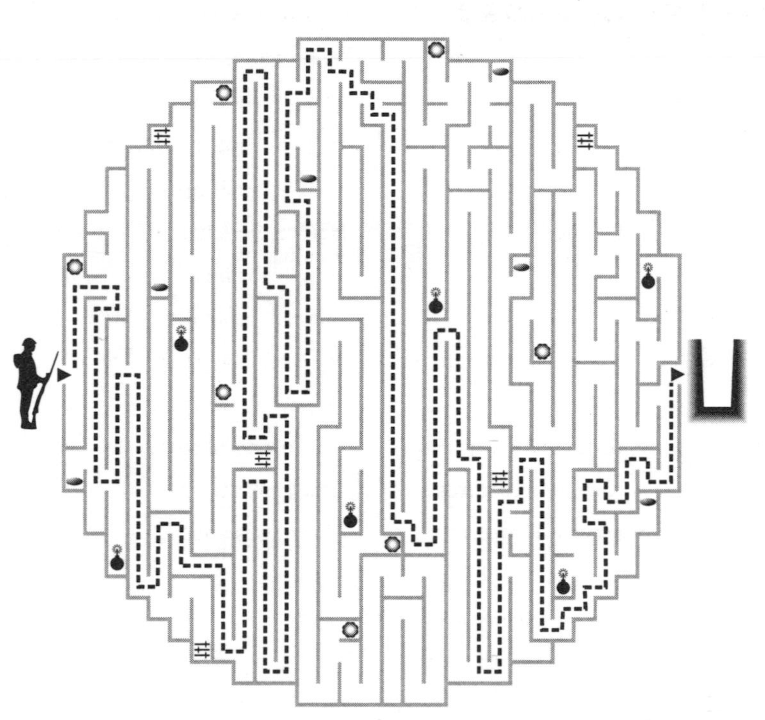

MONKEY PUZZLE

The Origin of Species by Charles Darwin, which promoted the theory of evolution by natural selection. The book's full title is *On the Origin of Species by Means of Natural Selection, or the Preservation of Favoured Races in the Struggle for Life.*

AFRICAN NUMBERS

C. More than 90 per cent

CITY NICKNAMES

City of 100 Spires	A nineteenth century mathematician counted them	Prague, Czech Republic
City of Light	Centre of the European Age of Enlightenment	Paris, France
Forbidden City	Royal palace complex	Beijing, China
Eternal City	The ancients believed the city would last for ever	Rome, Italy
Big Apple	Originally used to describe the city's horseracing tracks and races	New York City, USA
Venice of the North	A large number of canals	Amsterdam, the Netherlands
Big Smoke	Thick smogs due to pollution in the twentieth century	London, UK

POINT OUT THE PYRAMIDS

C. Merovingian France

WOMEN WHO MADE HISTORY

1. Pocahontas
2. Joan of Arc
3. Tomoe Gozen
4. Empress Wu (Wu Zetian)

REBELLIOUS THIRTEEN

Connecticut
Delaware
Georgia
Maryland
Massachusetts
New Hampshire
New Jersey
New York
North Carolina
Pennsylvania
South Carolina
Rhode Island
Virginia

EVENTS OF THE SECOND WORLD WAR

The Battle of El-Alamein	Egypt
The Blitz	UK
The biggest tank battle in history	Kursk, Russia
Pearl Harbor	Hawaii
A protracted battle for control of a monastery strongpoint	Monte Cassino, Italy
Anne Frank's refuge	Amsterdam

COUNTING THE STARS

The Maya.

TRAVELLERS' TALES

1. Henry Hudson
2. Christopher Columbus
3. Lao Tzu
4. Marco Polo

FASHION STATEMENTS

1. **False**. It was invented earlier in the twentieth century by Sun Yat-sen.
2. **True**. Two-piece swimming costumes were worn earlier in the twentieth century, but in 1946 the modern, skimpy bikini was introduced, partly to save materials.
3. **False**. He began to wear traditional clothes in solidarity with the many poor people of India.
4. **False**. It became known as the New Look.
5. **True**. He patented the style with his partner Jacob W. Davis.
6. **True**.
7. **True**. The corsets pushed women's breasts out to the front and pushed their hips backwards.
8. **False**. They were invented in the USA.
9. **True**. She wanted to produce something elegant and versatile, but economical so every woman could afford one.
10. **True**. She was a supporter of such 'rational' clothes for women.

A CRUCIAL BATTLE

The diagram shows the Battle of Stalingrad (23 August 1942 to 2 February 1943) in the USSR. The eventual Soviet victory there was a watershed event, with some historians believing it to be the turning point of the Second World War. The German front line in the East was pushed back and from then on the Nazis were in retreat in the East, while the Soviet army began to press on, unstoppable, until it reached Berlin. Germany lost its entire 6th Army, which was cut off and pinned down in Stalingrad. Despite Hitler's orders, the 6th Army surrendered. Troops had to be moved from the West to replace the losses. It was a massive morale boost for the Allies, particularly for the USSR, while Germany became demoralized.

INVADERS AND DICTATORS

They publicly burnt books that they disapproved of or were not interested in. In Nineveh and Alexandria entire libraries were burnt.

TABLE MANNERS

Spoons: very ancient versions have been found. Chopsticks and forks for personal use, rather than as cooking utensils, have been used from around the fourth century AD.

WHAT'S IN A NAME?

1. Genghis Khan
2. The 1st Duke of Wellington
3. President Tito of Yugoslavia
4. Emperor Haile Selassie of Ethiopia
5. Stalin

NEW WORLD MAP

Romania

CHARLES THE GREAT

Emperor of the Romans (Holy Roman Emperor)

ROYAL CARPENTER

Peter the Great of Russia

LIBRARY LIST

Sweden

CLASSICAL MUSIC

The piano

SILHOUETTES

6. A. Stonehenge, *c.* 3000 BC
9. E. The Great Pyramid, *c.* 2560 BC
8. G. Peru's Nazca Plain Lines, 500 BC–AD 500
7. J. The Great Wall of China, 221 BC (this was when earlier, smaller walls were joined into one Great Wall)
5. C. The Colosseum, AD 70–80
1. F. Easter Island statues, 1100–1680
2. I. The Taj Mahal, 1632–1648
4. B. The heyday of Native Canadian totem poles, 1800s (after metal tools were introduced the custom flourished)
10. D. Sagrada Familia, 1882–
3. H. The Eiffel Tower, 1887–9

NATIONAL GROWTH

1. The Dutch Republic embarked upon land reclamation through dykes and drainage.
2. As part of a wider conflict, Britain defeated France in Canada and took control of all France's colonies there.
3. The USA made the Louisiana Purchase, buying from France that country's claim to settle in a huge area of North America.

EUROPE IN 1812

The map (opposite) shows how much of Europe was ruled by or influenced by Napoleon Bonaparte, and how few countries actively opposed him.

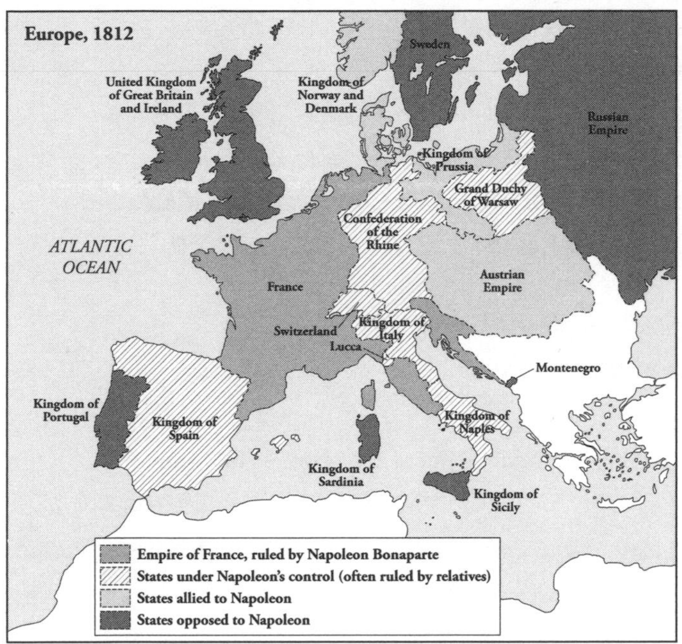

HISTORICAL QUOTES

1. E. Napoleon Bonaparte
2. D. Karl Marx
3. B. Ovid
4. A. Confucius
5. C. Winston Churchill

ITALY BEFORE UNIFICATION

The fictitious Bolognese Principality

SIGNIFICANT OTHERS

1. Pharaoh Akhenaten
2. Alexander the Great
3. Louis VII of France; Henry II of England
4. No one – Elizabeth I never married
5. Shah Jahan, who built the Taj Mahal to house her tomb
6. Pierre Curie

WAR AND PEACE

1. C. American Revolutionary Colonel William Prescott
2. D. Native American Nez Perce leader Chief Joseph
3. B. Second World War U.S. General Douglas MacArthur
4. A. Genghis Khan

DOT TO DOT

The hummingbird drawing of the Nazca Plain Lines, Peru.

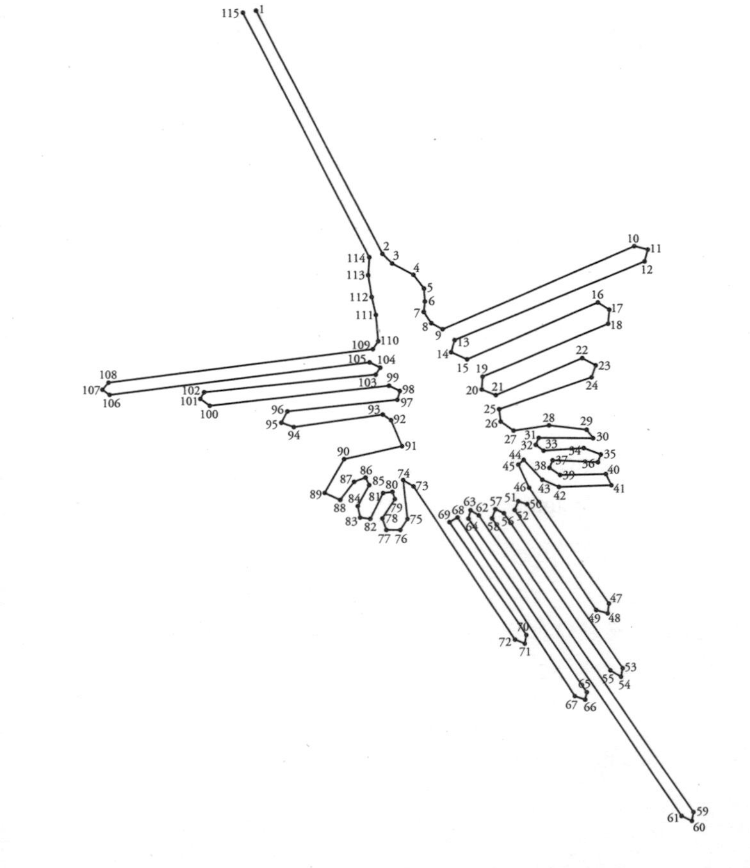

ARTISTIC ORDER

3. The Pyramid of the Sun, *c.* AD 200
5. Edinburgh Castle, 1130
6. Ming vases, *c.*1400 to 1644 (the Ming dynasty ruled China from 1368 to 1644 but typical Ming porcelain was first developed in the early 1400s)
1. The *Mona Lisa*, 1503
4. *Sunflowers,* 1887-9
2. *The Scream*, 1893

ODD ONE OUT

The Solvay Conference: an agreement by international scientists on how to deal with the new area of quantum physics. All the others are treaties, alliances or agreements between nations.

AMERICAN PRESIDENTS

2. George Washington
6. Abraham Lincoln
3. Ulysses S. Grant
1. Theodore Roosevelt
5. Franklin D. Roosevelt
4. Dwight D. Eisenhower

LINKED IN

They were all murdered and their killers have never been definitely identified.

AN ENGLISH MAZE

The maze is at Hampton Court Palace in the London borough of Richmond-Upon-Thames. There are a few different routes but here is the quickest.

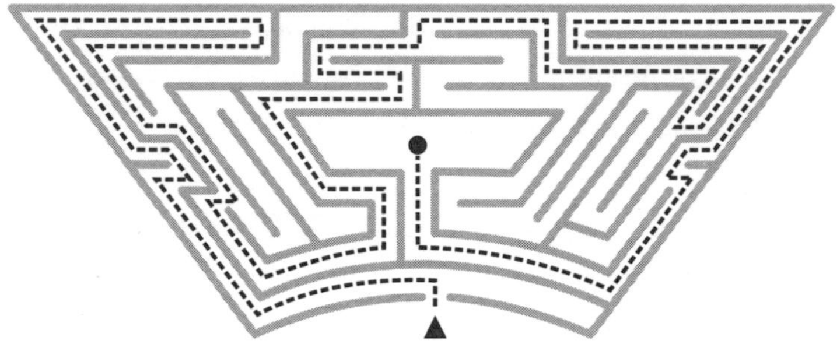

TRADITIONS

1. Japan
2. Indonesia, but also other parts of South East and East Asia
3. Italy
4. The Netherlands
5. West Africa
6. Scotland
7. France
8. Australia

INITIAL VALUES

1. *Schutzstaffel* (Protection Squad), the Nazi paramilitary
2. *Kuomintang* (nowadays usually *Guomindang*), the Chinese Nationalist Party
3. The People's Republic of China, the communist state
4. Federal Bureau of Investigation
5. Union of Soviet Socialist Republics

TEETOTAL YEARS

Prohibition.
C. 32,000

DYNASTY

Assyria, Ashur-uballit
Inca, Manco Capac
Guptan empire of India, Chandra
Austro-Hungarian, Franz Joseph
Han dynasty of China, Liu Bang

WHAT'S THE LINK?

A. They introduced reformed or new calendars.
B. They started or were the origin of disastrous fires: Pudding Lane is the street where the Great Fire of London began in 1666. Mother O'Leary's cow is believed to have caused the Great Chicago Fire in 1871 by kicking over a lantern in a barn. Roman general Scipio Aemilianus in North Africa destroyed the city of Carthage by fire at the end of the Third Punic War in 146 BC. When a Japanese priest in Edo attempted to burn a supposedly cursed kimono the wind blew sparks onto the wooden temple walls, causing the Great Fire of Meireki in 1657. Some 100,000 people are thought to have died and three-quarters of the city burnt down.

WAR PRODUCTION

Germany

ARTISTIC TIME TRAVEL

E. The Shang Dynasty in China was from about 1600 to 1046 BC
D. Chartres Cathedral was completed in 1220
C. The heyday of Benin

bronzes was between about 1550 and 1750

F. Beethoven wrote his *Moonlight Sonata* in 1801

B. The Pre-Raphaelite Brotherhood was founded in 1848

A. The Harlem Renaissance was in the 1920s

FOOTBALL PICTOGRAM

This illustrates the Christmas Truce in 1914, when soldiers from opposite sides mingled, exchanged prisoners and played football matches along the Western Front during the First World War.

MISSING WORDS

Musa
West
Sahara
salt
books
Islam
Mecca
elephants
gold
world
Spain
Battuta

A COMMON WEALTH

New South Wales
Queensland
South Australia
Tasmania
Victoria
Western Australia

New Zealand decided to go its own way and not join the new federation.

MONEY TALKS

C. 500 million marks

SCIENTIFIC EXILE

Werner Heisenberg, who did not have Jewish ancestry.

LIFE IS BETTER WITH …

4. Cornflakes, 1906
5. The Model T Ford, 1908
2. The bra, 1910
3. The roadside cat's eye reflector, 1934
1. Nylon, 1935

AN ANCIENT MAZE

This is the solution. This type of maze often gives you no option other than to wind round following every path within it.

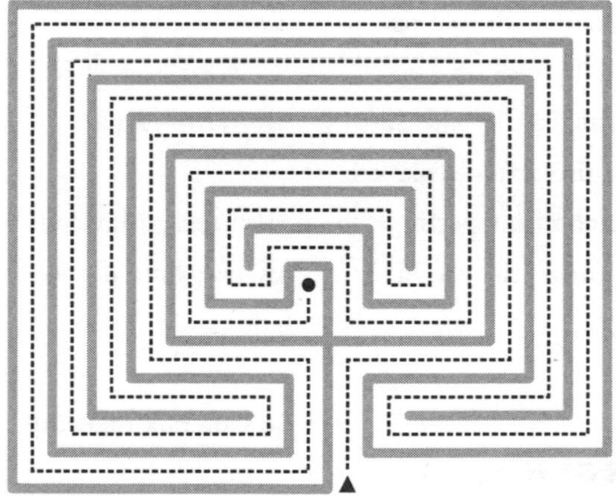

1. A labyrinth
2. The Cretan or Minoan civilization
3. The minotaur
4. The *labrys*, or double-sided axe of the Minoan culture, is probably the origin of the name of this type of maze.

A NOVEL APPROACH TO HISTORY

D. Written in the fourteenth century; set in the Three Kingdoms Period in China from AD 120 to 280
A. 1844; the early seventeenth century during the reign of French King Louis XIII when Cardinal de Richelieu was First Minister
E. 1859; 1775–92, before and during the French Revolution
C. Finished in 1868; the Napoleonic Era, specifically the 1812 invasion of Russia by Napoleon Bonaparte
B. 1895; the American Civil War of 1861–5

CANADIAN CONFEDERATION

The Province of Canada, Nova Scotia and New Brunswick. The Province of Canada divided into Ontario and Québec.

THIRTY YEARS OF TERROR

1. C. Disputes over the division of wealth from the Americas
2. The lands of the Holy Roman Empire in central Europe
3. Sweden and France
4. France

NATURAL DISASTER

In the 1930s, dust storms devastated the prairies of the USA causing what is known as the 'Dust Bowl'.

Although this was a natural disaster brought about by wind and drought, it was aggravated by misguided farming practices in which farmers dug out all the natural prairie grass that fixed both the water and topsoil in place on the plains.

The Dust Bowl added to the problems caused by the Great Depression, a global financial crisis that began in the USA following the Wall Street Crash of 1929, bank failures and other economic problems.

It was only when the Second World War broke out that industry was revitalized and men found paid work in the armed services.

THE THIRD ROME

A. Moscow

ANCIENT THINKER

Aristotle. He was referring to the death of the philosopher Socrates, who in 399 BC, having been accused of impiety and corruption by the Athenian authorities, was forced to take a deadly dose of poison.

FACTIONS

C. Those representatives who supported change sat on the left-hand side.

DEATH BY EVERY MEANS POSSIBLE

Diseases to which they had no resistance, particularly smallpox.

FIRST WORDS

C. '*Mr Watson, come here. I want to see you.*' They were spoken by Alexander Graham Bell on 10 March 1876, to his assistant Thomas Watson.

MISSING AMENITIES?

True.
Toilets were not added until 1768, 144 years after the palace was begun. In its early days, commodes overflowed and waste could drip down through ceilings.

FILM NIGHT, PART 2

1. She was a Dutch-Jewish woman
2. Apartheid, an Afrikaans word for 'separateness'
3. A medieval Crusader knight in *The Seventh Seal*
4. The Colosseum in Rome
5. The Japanese airplane designer Horikoshi Jiro and his two Second World War planes: the Mitsubishi A5M and the Mitsubishi A6M Zero

ABSOLUTE ADVANCES

The use of torture and serfdom.

A GAP IN THE MAP

Poland, and A. Jan III Sobieski defeated the Ottomans at the siege of Vienna in 1683.

MISSING TREASURES

Route 1 leads to (B)
Route 2 leads to (C)
Route 3 leads to (A)

A. The 'Crown Jewels' of Ireland, the regalia of the Order of St Patrick, stolen in 1907 from Dublin Castle, Ireland.
B. The Honjo Masamune samurai sword of Japan, lost in the chaos after the Second World War.
C. The Imperial Fabergé eggs, several of which went missing from Russia during the Russian Revolution.

SCHOOL'S OUT FOR SOME

B. Only the nobility

AGE OF DISCOVERY

Portugal and the Netherlands

INDUSTRIAL REASONS

C. In fact, it was relatively easy to move raw materials and goods around Britain since it had a temperate climate, plenty of rivers and canals and did not have serious geographical barriers such as deserts or huge mountains.

DANCING YEARS

C. Russia in the late nineteenth century

SPOT THE DIFFERENCE

British politician Winston Churchill.

The changes are:

- **The hat band pattern**
- **A feather in the hat**
- **The tie**
- **The cane**
- **Left-hand sleeve length**
- **Button shape**
- **The watch**
- **The shape of his badge**
- **One finger in the air**
- **The mobile phone**

The anachronism is a mobile phone instead of a pocket handkerchief.

LITERATE HISTORY

'The first novel'	*The Tale of Genji*	Murasaki Shikibu
'The first modern novel'	*Don Quixote*	Miguel de Cervantes
'The first science-fiction novel'	*Frankenstein*	Mary Shelley
'Masterpiece of Realism'	*Madame Bovary*	Gustave Flaubert
'Greatest writer in the English language'	*Complete Works*	William Shakespeare
Influential slave narrative	*Life of Frederick Douglass*	Frederick Douglass
Italian epic poem	*Divine Comedy*	Dante Alighieri
'Greatest work in the German language'	*Faust*	Johann Wolfgang von Goethe
'Nihilism, damnation, redemption'	*Crime and Punishment*	Fyodor Dostoyevsky
Foundation of modern fantasy	*The Lord of the Rings*	J.R.R. Tolkien

MASS MARKETING

Affordable sports shoes with rubber soles, now often called trainers. They became known as sneakers in the USA because the rubber sole allowed people to 'sneak' around quietly.

BUY AND SELL

A. Amsterdam

TAXING TIMES

1. Men's beards
2. Salt
3. Windows
4. Cooking oil
5. The Stamp Act, which required revenue stamps to be put on all printed paper

GIVE AND TAKE

Potlatch, a ceremony which served as a display of wealth and rank

DUTCH DIVISION

Belgium

ANCIENT WONDERS

1. The Colossus of Rhodes
2. The Great Pyramid (Pyramid of Khufu) at Giza
3. The Hanging Gardens of Babylon
4. The Lighthouse of Alexandria
5. The Mausoleum at Halicarnassus
6. The Statue of Zeus
7. The Temple of Artemis

Only the Great Pyramid still remains.

A RATHER EXPENSIVE CHILD SUPPORT BILL

Genghis Khan

WASTE NOT

Natural gas

D-DAY BEACHES

1. 6 June 1944
2. From left to right: Utah, Omaha, Gold, Juno, Sword
3. From left to right: the USA, the USA, Britain, Canada, Britain
4. (A) The U.S. 82nd Airborne Division; (B) The British 6th Airborne Division
5. Men from Australia, Belgium, Czechoslovakia, Denmark, France, Greece, the Netherlands, New Zealand, Norway and Poland all took part in the Normandy invasion.
6. Operation Overlord and Operation Neptune
7. American General Dwight D. Eisenhower. In 1953 he took office as U.S. president.

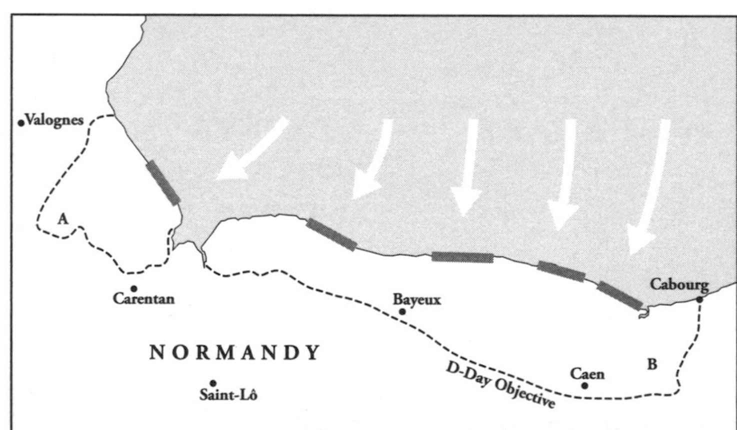

LINKS ACROSS TIME

Baths: Archimedes is said to have had his 'Eureka' moment and realized the physical law of buoyancy while in a bath.

According to one account, Agamemnon was killed in a bath.

Jean-Paul Marat was assassinated while taking a medicinal bath.

EVERYDAY ITEMS

Some form of flushing toilets

RIGHT TO RULE

Charles X, from 1824 to 1830.

He abdicated since he believed in an absolute monarchy which the French people no longer accepted.

OLDEST EVENT

B. The Taiping Rebellion began in China in 1850

ESCAPEES

A. State officials were required to help capture runaway slaves and return them to the slave-owner

INDUSTRIAL EXPANSION

The part of the European Low Countries that became Belgium

A ROYAL FLEET

Piracy

RUSSIAN RULERS

Romanov

A COMMON TOUCH, PART 2

They all had red hair or red beards.

A TIMELINE

C. Babylonian

TERRACOTTA TOMB

A. Horses
C. More than 7,000 figures

FIRST FASCISTS

A. War veterans

REVOLUTIONARY SLAVES

Haiti (Saint-Domingue), from 1791 to 1804. The successful general was Toussaint L'Ouverture who died in 1803.

GLOBAL LINK

For a few years they were contemporaneous rulers

POST-WAR CHANGES

1. The USA
2. Yugoslavia
3. India, becoming India and Pakistan
4. Israel

PRE-REVOLUTIONARY TIMES

Aristocracy, clergy and commoners.

The aristocrats and clergy did not pay taxes.

SHARED EXPERIENCES

The first group were all held hostage when children for

political reasons. (At the age of twelve Attila became a hostage at the court of Roman Emperor Honorius.) Theodoric and James I were held hostage for political reasons when adults.

The final group were kidnapped and held captive either for ransom, or in the case of Chiang Kai-shek, until he agreed to a ceasefire against the Communists in order to deal with the Japanese invasion of China.

CITY LINKS

Venice
The word 'ghetto' comes from the name of the Venetian district where Jewish people were forced to live in the Middle Ages. The word 'quarantine' comes from the Venetian dialect word for 'forty days', which, from the mid-fifteenth century, was the length of time that Venice required ships to wait before entering the city if they were suspected of carrying the plague. During the eighteenth century, Venetian citizens were required to wear masks when voting so they would be anonymous.

YEAR OF REVOLUTION

1. 1848
2. Italy, France, German States, Austria and Hungary
3. The UK, with the Chartist movement
4. *The Communist Manifesto* by Karl Marx and Friedrich Engels

TEN THOUSAND OR TWO?

Qin Shi Huangdi, the 'First Emperor' of China, the first of the Qin Dynasty that created a united China.

CRIMINAL CONFERENCE

The Nazis decided to systematically murder every Jewish person in Europe through dedicated death camps.

ASSASSINATED PRESIDENTS

Abraham Lincoln in 1865
James A. Garfield in 1881
William McKinley in 1901

Lincoln's son Robert Todd Lincoln was with his father when Abraham Lincoln was fatally shot; as secretary of war he went to meet his president just as James Garfield was shot; and he was at the same event as McKinley when that president was assassinated.

WHAT LINKS?

They were all founded by Vikings or Norsemen

MAORI CUSTOMS

A tattoo

LITTLE WONDER

The transistor

WHO WAS SHE?

Harriet Tubman

KOREAN CONQUEST

Japan

FIRST COLONY

B. St. John's, Newfoundland, in 1583

MONGOL MAZE

The paths that avoid hills and will keep you ahead of the Mongols are shown opposite.

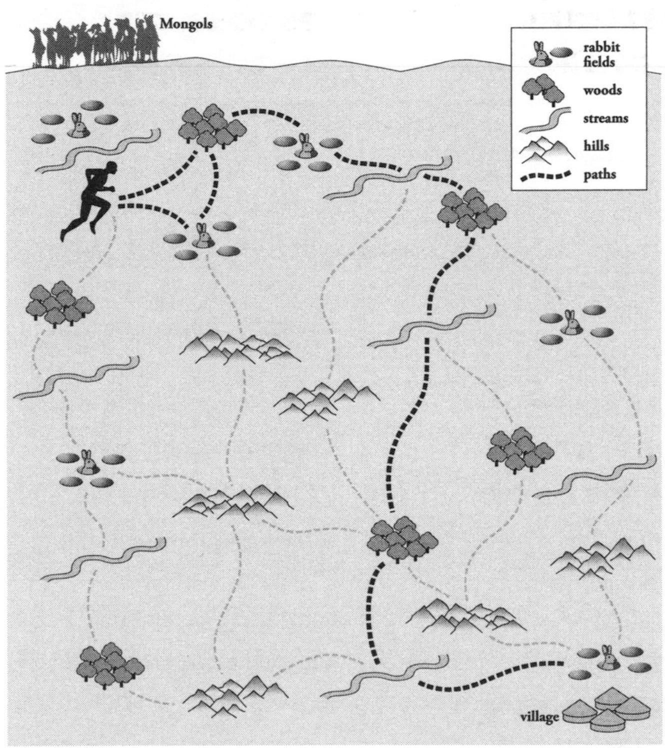

A RARE DEFEAT

Attila the Hun, who was defeated by a combined force of Romans and Visigoths

BYZANTINE FACTIONS

The mobs were supporters of the rival chariot-racing teams, the Blues and the Greens. In AD 532 the mob violence culminated in the Nika Riots, when the opposing factions united in a revolt in Constantinople against Emperor Justinian I. The rioters based themselves in the Hippodrome, the city's racing track, and after five days Justinian sent armed troops to massacre them. Up to 30,000 people were killed and the days of mob rule were ended.

JAMAICAN HEROINE

Maroons, and Queen Nanny

LAND GRAB

C. (Actually 87 per cent)

THE DEALER

A. A Square Deal

A CANADIAN HOME

Vikings from Greenland

ADVERTISING

Hollywood

PEOPLE OF THE YEAR

Mahatma (Mohandas) Gandhi, 1930
Pierre Laval, 1931
Franklin D. Roosevelt, 1932
Hugh S. Johnson, 1933
Franklin D. Roosevelt, 1934
Haile Selassie, 1935
Wallis Simpson, 1936
Chiang Kai-shek and Madame Chiang (Soong Meiling), 1937
Adolf Hitler, 1938
Joseph Stalin, 1939

GET AHEAD

B. Olmec

FIRST THINGS FIRST

China. Among other things: abacus (Chinese abacus, with upper and lower sections), acupuncture, belt drive, blast furnace, chopsticks, compass (magnetic), fireworks, gunpowder (and rockets, bombs, cannon, etc), lacquer, kites, paper (including paper money), porcelain, printing, rudder, seismometer, silk weaving, the wheelbarrow…

WHO WERE THEY?

The Incas of western South America. The knots were known as *quipus* or *khipus*.

SIX DEGREES OF SEPARATION

One possible solution for six links is:
Around 1275 **Marco Polo** arrived in China and met Kublai Khan, the Mongol emperor.
Kublai Khan corresponded with Pope Clement IV.
Pope Clement IV was a sponsor of English theologian and alchemist Roger Bacon.
Roger Bacon was popularly held to be a wizard who had invented a bronze head that could answer any question. This featured in the popular comic play *The Honorable Historie of Frier Bacon and Frier Bongay*, written by Robert Greene around 1589.
Robert Greene wrote the first reference to **William Shakespeare** as a playwright, contemptuously calling him an 'upstart Crow' and 'Shake-scene'.
The single link could be Shakespeare's play *The Merchant of Venice*, since Marco Polo was a merchant from Venice.

AN AMERICAS SEQUENCE

Places where Christopher Columbus landed during his four voyages to the Americas.

FIRST WRITINGS

A. Early Chinese characters
B. Linear A from the Minoan culture on Crete

C. Egyptian hieroglyphs
D. Cuneiform from Mesopotamia (Sumeria/Babylonia/Assyria)
E. Norse runes
F. Pictograms from Indus Valley seals

Linear A script and the Indus Valley pictograms have not yet been deciphered.

RESISTANCE WAS NOT FUTILE

A. Attempted to assassinate Hitler
B. Coded messages broadcast by the BBC

WHO SAID?

Captain Lawrence Edward Grace Oates in 1912 towards the end of the British Antarctic Expedition. Led by Robert Falcon Scott, it ended with the deaths of every expedition member. Oates said this as, sick and slowing the team down, he left the tent and walked into a blizzard.

ODD ONE OUT: NORTH AMERICAN BATTLES

C. Guilford Court House, which was a battle in the American Revolution. The others were battles in the American Civil War.

NON-COMBATANTS

1. Accountants, to add up the loot, captives and areas of land conquered.
2. Historians, to record Alexander's achievements for posterity.
3. Engineers, to construct camps at the end of each day's march, as well as to build bridges and roads for the army's use.

ZONES OF INFLUENCE

1. Britain, France, the Soviet Union and the USA
2. Berlin lay in the Soviet

Union's zone, but the city was also divided into four areas run by Britain, France, the Soviet Union and the USA

3. The Berlin Airlift. The Soviet Union blockaded land and river access to the Western-run zones of Berlin, so Britain, France, the USA and allies such as Australia, Canada, New Zealand and South Africa flew supplies into the city.

SUCCESSFUL SISTERS

Vietnam

TOY STORIES

A. A painting on a Greek vase from 440 BC shows a boy playing with a yo-yo

A. Several toys have been found in the Indus Valley cities, including a monkey made to slide down a string or rod.

U.S. President Theodore (Teddy) Roosevelt

SUCCESSFUL STRATEGY

Blitzkrieg (translated as 'lightning war'). This involved a sudden, swift attack by a force of tanks, mobile artillery and mechanized infantry concentrated at one strategic point. The ground force would be covered from the air by dive bombers, all well coordinated by radio communications. The first attack would be backed up by more troops.

NAME THAT YEAR

1905

AN AFRICAN QUEEN

A. Nzinga

LAST OUTPOST

New Zealand. Possibly just 750 years ago, from Polynesia

A GROWING QUESTION

1. C. Tulip
2. B. Cotton
3. D. Cinnamon
4. E. Rose (the Wars of the Roses)
5. A. Laurel

POISON IN THE BUNKER

A. Eva Braun's fictitious cat Mizzi. She had two dogs, which were shot after Braun and Hitler committed suicide.

ANIMAL LINKS

They were all hunted to extinction by human beings except for the buffalo in North America, which narrowly escaped extinction.

WELL TRAVELLED

Viking raiders from Norway, Sweden or Denmark

TRADE ROUTES

1. Sumeria in Mesopotamia and the Indus Valley cities in northern India / Pakistan
2. The Incense Route, and on overland routes goods were carried on camels
3. The Silk Road. The Mongols imposed strict laws in the lands they conquered, so patrolled against bandits, making travel along the trade routes safer than before.
4. Buffalo 'traces', the paths made by migrating buffalo

NORTH/SOUTH DIVIDE

1. The War Between the States, the War for Southern Independence, the War of the Rebellion, the War to

Preserve the Union, the War of Northern Aggression, Mr Lincoln's War, Mr Davis's War

2. The Confederacy was formed of Alabama, Arkansas, Florida, Georgia, Louisiana, Mississippi, North Carolina, South Carolina, Tennessee, Texas and Virginia.
3. The Union comprised California, Connecticut, Illinois, Indiana, Iowa, Kansas, Maine, Massachusetts, Michigan, Minnesota, Nevada, New Hampshire, New Jersey, New York, Ohio, Oregon, Pennsylvania, Rhode Island, Vermont, Washington D.C. and Wisconsin.
4. Maryland, Delaware, Kentucky, West Virginia and Missouri were called Border States since they were slave-owning, but did not secede from the Union. Kentucky at first remained neutral but later came fully under Union control, as did Maryland and Delaware. West Virginia was formed from part of Virginia and became a Union state in 1863. Missouri was more divided, with both a Unionist and a Confederate government, though it never formally seceded from the United States.

HOUSE OF DREAD

Workhouses, where destitute people were housed but families were split up and conditions could be appalling.

HISTORY IS BUNK

American industrialist Henry Ford

OOPS, YOUR TIME MACHINE IS BROKEN

C. 30 BC
B. 1815
A. 1842–43

BRAZILIAN EXPORT

Coffee

PARTITION OF AFRICA

1. The Scramble for Africa
2. The Berlin Conference in 1884, when European would-be colonizers tried to reach an agreement on partitioning Africa to avoid coming into conflict with each other
3. A. 0

ANCIENT SOUTH ASIA

B. Plazas for human sacrifices

NORTHERN REBELS

The Harrying of the North.
C. All of them

FIRST JOURNEYS

1. **Christopher Columbus**, first Atlantic crossing (1492)

2. **Vasco da Gama**, first sea route from Europe to Asia, (1497–99)

3. **Ferdinand Magellan**, first circumnavigation of the world (1519 to 1522, died in the Philippines in 1521)

Map shown below

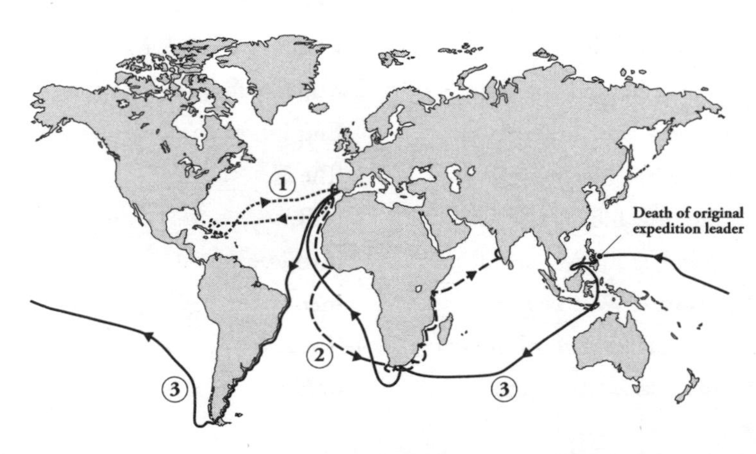

INDEPENDENCE DATE

Indonesia

GETTYSBURG SPEECH

C. 2 minutes
equal
people
people
Earth

IRISH RULE

Vikings

PREHISTORIC BUILDERS

1. Göbekli Tepe in south-east Turkey, begun about 9130 BC
2. Çatalhöyük
3. Jericho
4. It is the only surviving stone circle with trilithons: horizontal lintel stones capping two uprights; it is the only one where upright stones were linked into a circle by tongue-and-groove joints; it is the only one where mortise and tenon joints were used, to join the lintels to the uprights.

ANTI-SLAVERY

The USA in 1865
Cuba in 1886
Brazil in 1888

MILITARY MIGHT

1. The second Mongol / Chinese invasion of Japan in 1281
2. The 1683 Battle of Vienna, when European cavalry helped defeat the Ottoman Empire's siege of Vienna.
3. The German / Axis invasion of Russia in 1941, initially involving about 3.2 million men
4. The Allied D-Day invasion of Normandy in 1944

5. The German siege of Leningrad, lasting 872 days, though known as the 900-Day Siege
6. The Germans' initial advance into Russia, which achieved 200 miles in one week
7. The British Indian Army, which eventually numbered 2.5 million volunteers
8. The Battle of Stalingrad, involving about 2.2 million combatants and resulting in 1.8-2 million deaths, casualties or captives

DUAL NATIONALITIES

A. French; he was General Jean Bernadotte
B. German, her father was Prince of Anhalt-Zerbst
C. Austrian, she was the daughter of Empress Maria Theresa and Holy Roman Emperor Francis I
D. Dutch
E. Mongol

NEW JOBS FOR OLD

A. Railways

WOMEN WARRIORS

B. The purely fictional Mayan princess Itzel-Kuk

WORLD FIRSTS

1. Sumeria.
2. It was known to its people as Kengir, which means 'The Civilized Land'.
3. It was based in Mesopotamia, the land between the Tigris and Euphrates rivers in what is effectively modern Iraq.
4. B. City-states
5. The Akkadian Empire, named after the city of Akkad that was chosen as its capital city. The empire was forged by Sargon of Kish.

POPULATION PRESSURE

The Achaemenid Empire or first Persian Empire from 550 to 330 BC. Around 480 BC it ruled over about 49.4 million people, from Central Asia to the Mediterranean, North Africa, and Thrace and Macedonia in Europe. This is thought to be about 44 per cent of the world's population at the time.

COMMON GROUND

They are the end points or the meeting places for the first trans-continental railways in their respective countries / continents. (Paris and Constantinople were the original end points of the Orient Express, which while not technically a full trans-continental railway is often considered to be one.)

A MUCH-TRAVELLED GROUP

The Knights Hospitaller (the Order of Knights of the Hospital of St John of Jerusalem / the Knights of Malta / the Order of Saint John / the Sovereign Military Order of Malta / the St John Ambulance Brigade, and other modern groups)

TRUE OR FALSE?

False. They travelled from South East Asia.

WHAT DECADE IS THIS?

The 1780s

MASS DEATHS

The outbreak of plague known as the Black Death or Great Plague.

FREEDOM FIGHTERS

D. Ruling aristocrats of Spanish descent

AVIATION MILESTONE

The sound barrier

FIVE, FOUR, THREE, TWO, ONE

5 Firsts

1. The Holy Roman Empire or Carolingian Empire, founded by Charlemagne in 800, which lasted in varying forms until 1806
2. Qin Shi Huangdi, the 'First Emperor' of China, the first Qin emperor
3. John Logie Baird
4. New South Wales
5. Orville and Wilbur Wright

4 Seconds

1. John Adams
2. French
3. The German Empire, lasting from 1871 to 1918, effectively founded by the Prussian leaders King Wilhelm I and Prime Minister Otto von Bismarck, with Wilhelm becoming the first emperor or Kaiser of Germany
4. The nineteenth century, lasting from 1848 to 1851

3 Thirds

1. From January 1933 to May 1945, founded by Adolf Hitler, commonly called Nazi Germany
2. Beijing
3. Russia

2 Fourths

1. Mary I
2. Korea

1 Fifth

The protection against self-incrimination clause, which means defendants in a criminal trial can refuse to answer questions that might incriminate them.

SNAKES AND LADDERS

1. 6 - 2 = 4
2. 7 (Seven Years' War)
3. IV or 4
4. 3
5. 1 (1918 - 100 [Years' War] - 30 [Years' War] = 1788).
   The French Revolution began in 1789, one year later.
6. 3

64	63	62	61	60	59	58	57
49	50	51	52	53	54	55	56
48	47	46	45	44	43	42	41
33	34	35	36	37	38	39	40
32	31	30	29	28	27	26	25
17	18	19	20	21	22	23	24
16	15	14	13	12	11	10	9
1	2	3	4	5	6	7	8

SHOOTING GALLERY?

True.
The sharpshooter was Annie Oakley.

WHAT LINKS?

They were all involved in developing laws. Hammurabi codified laws and had them inscribed on stones that were placed around the country; Charlemagne centralized law in his empire; Justinian and Napoleon developed law codes; King John signed the Magna Carta, a charter of rights that became part of English statute law.

MUGHAL INDIA

1. Babur, descended from Genghis Khan and the Turco-Mongol leader Timur (Tamerlane)
2. Aurangzeb
3. The British East India Company

CHINESE REVOLUTION

B. Sun Yat-sen

VOTES FOR WOMEN

New Zealand, 1893
Norway, 1913
Denmark and Iceland, 1915
Russia, 1917
Canada, 1918

Australia in 1902 and Finland in 1906

PLAIN DEALING

1. Scythians
2. The Great Wall of China
3. Parthians
4. Mongols
5. Many inventions to do with horses: stirrups, bits and bridles, etc, and possibly the original domestication of horses.

HORRIBLE DEATHS

False.
The First World War was the first major conflict in which more soldiers died from fighting rather than from infections and diseases.

VICTORIA'S CHILDREN

This is just a simplified diagram of the many links forged by the children of Queen Victoria of Britain.

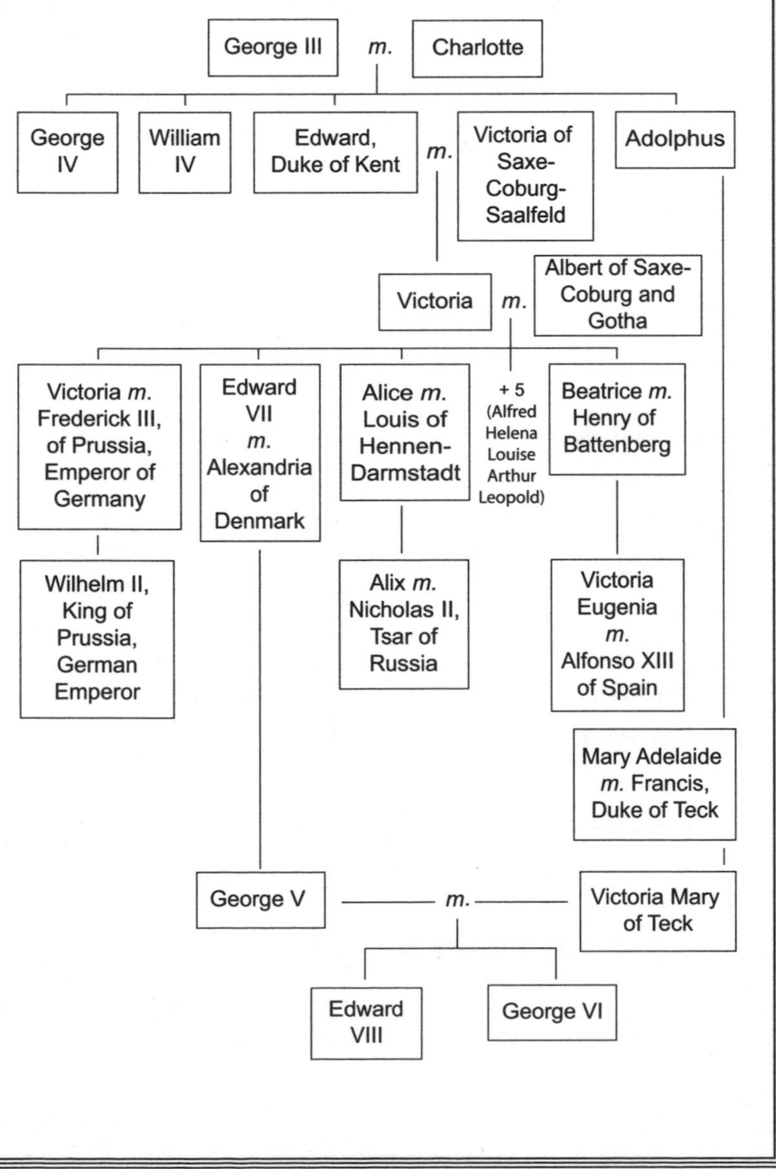

OLDEST RULERS

Japan.

The Japanese Imperial House traditionally traces its origin to 660 BC, and there is confirmed evidence for a line stretching back to around AD 500.

FLYING ACES

Five

DO YOU KNOW YOUR ANCESTORS?

1. Tanzania
2. Russia
3. Germany
4. Indonesia
5. South Africa
6. China
7. Canada, USA, Mexico

BALTIC TRADE

1. The Hanseatic League, also known as the Hanse or Hansa
2. Timber
3. Lübeck

UNIVERSAL DECLARATION

The United Nations

INTERRUPTED

The Olympic Games

A MERGER

Libya

THE TALE OF NEFERTARI

Great
I
Ozymandias
Kadesh
peace treaty
Turkey
sun
hieroglyphics

queen
Queens
death / the afterlife

REVOLUTIONARY TIMES

Russia

HUMAN RIGHTS

The Cyrus Cylinder, a clay cylinder inscribed in 539 BC on the order of Cyrus the Great, the founder of the Achaemenid or First Persian Empire. In it he declared that there should be no slavery in his empire, that all the different peoples were equal, and they enjoyed freedom of religion.

Unlike many conquerors, Cyrus did not conduct widespread massacres of vanquished populations. When he conquered the city of Babylon in 539 BC he left the city unmolested, even the temples, which most conquerors at the time would have destroyed as a sign of superiority. He also allowed the Jewish captives in Babylon to return to Judea.

CULTURAL WORKS

Christina Rossetti – *Goblin Market* – poetry
Pablo Picasso – Rose Period – painting
Pyotr Ilyich Tchaikovsky – *Swan Lake* – ballet
Erich Maria Remarque – *All Quiet on the Western Front* – literature
François-Auguste-René Rodin – *The Age of Bronze* – sculpture

OLYMPIC BUBBLE

Berlin. African-American athlete Jesse Owens, who won four gold medals for sprints and the long jump.

ATTACK PLAN

The Zulus. It was known as the 'buffalo horns' formation.

ROMAN SOLDIERS

1. 80
2. 100
3. A legion
4. A century was smaller, with six centuries forming a cohort
5. 10 cohorts (including one extra large cohort) formed a legion
6. Cavalry

DYNAMIC AWARDS

The Nobel Prizes. Alfred Nobel patented dynamite and gelignite.

ODD CULTURE

Impressionism, which began in the nineteenth century. All the others are twentieth-century movements.

EMPIRE STATE

The empire is that of Alexander the Great, encompassing Macedonia and his conquests of the Persian Empire, Egypt, and in Central Asia as far east as the Punjab.

PLAYS WELL WITH OTHERS

A. Football (soccer)
(*Which was much rougher in the past*)

OLD CITIES, NEW CITIES

1. New York
2. St Petersburg, Petrograd and Leningrad
3. Tokyo in Japan
4. Edinburgh
5. Mexico City

LASTING CONFLICT

The Cold War

PAINFUL PAINTING

The strategic aerial bombing of the Spanish town of Guernica during the Spanish Civil War

MUSICAL FIRST

C. The first solid-bodied electrical guitar

NO GOLD MEDAL

Darts

ARTS AND CRAFTS TIMELINE

9. Lascaux cave paintings, *c.*17,000 years ago
8. The city of Great Zimbabwe, eleventh century to fifteenth century
4. *The Garden of Earthly Delights* by Hieronymus Bosch, 1490–1510
6. Michelangelo's statue of David, 1501
7. *The Night Watch* by Rembrandt, 1640
5. *The Great Wave* by Hokusai, 1829–33
10. *Whistler's Mother* by James MacNeill Whistler, 1871
1. Claude Monet's *Water Lilies* series, 1896–1920
2. The heyday of trench art was during the First World War, 1914–18
3. *American Gothic* by Grant Wood, 1930

INDEPENDENCE NOW

India; Mahatma Gandhi

RIOTOUS BALLET

Igor Stravinsky's *The Rite of Spring*

GIANT ENCOUNTER

A. Giant panda

THE TERRIBLE TRENCHES

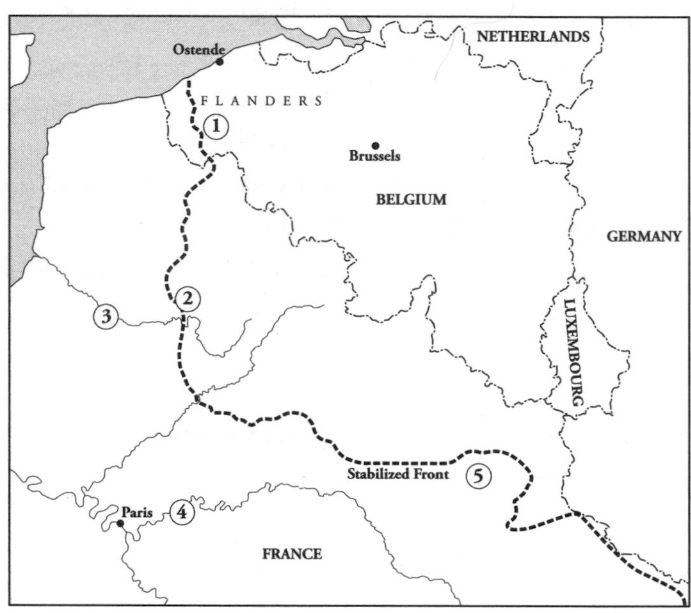

Battles:

1. Passchendaele (Ypres 3)
2. Somme
3. Amiens
4. Marne 1
5. Verdun

The date order was:

Marne 1, 6 to 12 September 1914

Verdun, 21 February to 18 December 1916

Somme, 1 July to 18 November 1916

Passchendaele (Ypres 3), 31 July to 10 November 1917

Amiens, 8 to 11 August 1918

EUROPEAN RECOVERY

B) The Marshall Plan

MUSIC TO GROW UP WITH

Peter and the Wolf by Sergey Prokofiev

HOUSE OF WISDOM

Baghdad in modern Iraq

BUILDING THE PAST

Ur – Great Ziggurat – *c.* 2050–2030 BC
Acropolis – Temple to Athena – 447–438 BC
Vitruvius – *On Architecture* – *c.* 50–15 BC
Mont-Saint-Michel – Romanesque / Gothic – Eleventh to sixteenth centuries
Filippo Brunelleschi – Renaissance – 1400s
Amritsar – Golden Temple – 1604
Crystal Palace – New industrial materials, e.g. cast iron –1851
Bavaria – King Ludwig II's fairy-tale castles – 1869–86
Chicago – First skyscraper – 1884–5
Walter Gropius – Bauhaus – 1919–33
Chrysler Building – Art deco – 1930
Le Corbusier – Villa Savoye – 1931

A MATTER OF GRAVITY

Galileo is thought to have used the Leaning Tower of Pisa for his experiment

ODD ONE OUT

Towton, which took place in 1461 during the civil conflict the Wars of the Roses. All the others were battles in the English Civil Wars (British Civil Wars or Wars of the Three Kingdoms) in the seventeenth century.

WHOSE FAMILY IS THIS?

The Habsburg family ruling Austria-Hungary and Spain. Several generations had the 'Habsburg Jaw', a large and protruding chin.

MEDICAL BREAKTHROUGHS

Breakthrough in smallpox inoculation	Edward Jenner	1796
Anaesthetics	William Morton	1846
Epidemiology / method of cholera infection	John Snow	1854
Germ theory of disease	Louis Pasteur	1857
Disinfectants	Joseph Lister	1860s
X-rays	Wilhelm Röntgen	1895
Psychoanalytic theory	Sigmund Freud	1895
Aspirin	Felix Hoffmann	1899
Blood groups / safe blood transfusions	Karl Landsteiner	1901
Discovery of radium	Marie Curie	1902
Iron lung	Philip Drinker	1927
Chemotherapy	Jane C. Wright	From 1949

THE RED FLAG

The union of agricultural and industrial workers

OIL!

It was in Iran, the first major find in the Middle East.

ODD MUSICAL STYLE

Calypso, which developed in Trinidad in the seventeenth century, while the other musical styles developed in the USA in the nineteenth or twentieth centuries.

BEWARE THE WARRIORS

1. Russian noblemen, originally the leaders of the Russian princes' armies.
2. Irregular soldiers of the Ottoman Empire, drawn from all its ethnic groups but primarily Albanians, Circassians and Kurds.
3. Vikings who wore animal skins instead of armour and probably worked themselves into a trance or frenzy before battle.

OLDEST PARLIAMENT

A. The Althing of Iceland, founded in AD 930

HEARTFELT QUOTE

Queen Elizabeth I of England, rallying the English forces to prepare to repel the invasion by the Spanish Armada in 1588.

DEBUT APPEARANCE

Walt Disney's cartoon character Mickey Mouse

HELP THE HISTORIAN

A and C lead to a book

DEADLY WEAPON

The longbow

CAPITAL CHOICE

C.

ONE YEAR, MANY EVENTS

The year was 1600 so it was technically the last year of the sixteenth century

SAILING THROUGH HISTORY

1. India Armadas
Trade fleets from Portugal to Asia and back from 1497 to 1511.

2. The First Fleet
The fleet carrying the British convicts, settlers, marines, etc. who founded the first colony in Australia. Leaving England on 13 May 1787, it arrived in Botany Bay on 15 January 1788.

3. The Triangular Trade and the Middle Passage
The three-leg Atlantic slave trade between the late sixteenth and early nineteenth centuries. First, European ships took mainly manufactured trade goods to Africa; then, on the middle journey, enslaved Africans were transported to the American colonies or to the Caribbean. The ships then carried primarily raw materials back to Europe.

4. Silver Fleets
Also called the West Indies Fleets, they were the convoys bringing goods and treasure to Spain from its lands in the Americas from 1566 to 1790.

5. Sea Beggars
The Dutch rebel navy who

fought against Spanish rule from the late sixteenth century.

6. Ming Treasure Fleets
Seven huge exploratory expeditions launched by the Chinese Yongle Emperor. They were led by Admiral Zheng He between 1405 and 1433. Carrying treasure as gifts, they expanded Chinese influence and authority as well as knowledge of the world.

7. Sea Peoples
Maritime raiders who terrorized the south-east Mediterranean coastlines from around 1276 BC. Ramesses III of Egypt destroyed them in 1178 BC.

8. The Great Tea Race
A competition between the clippers bringing tea from China to Britain in the nineteenth century. The rivalry to be the first ship to arrive with the new season's crop culminated in a prize race conducted in 1866.

YOUNG TURKS

B. The lack of a constitution

ODD ONE OUT

Tanagra, which was a battle in the Peloponnesian Wars between Athens and Sparta in Greece. The others were battles in the Greco-Persian Wars.

SOCIAL REFORMS

B. Working hours were NOT reduced to eight hours a day

WHOSE REPUBLIC?

Germany

ODD PHILOSOPHY OUT

Metaphysics, which was explored in most ancient cultures

WHAT'S THE LINK?

Although they were all at one time important and influential states, they all lost their independent status and were subsumed into other countries

OLDEST TROPHY

A. The America's Cup, for yachting, was first awarded in 1851 and is the oldest international sporting trophy
B. The Jules Rimet Trophy for world cup football (soccer) was awarded from 1930 (named after Jules Rimet in 1946) until 1970
C. The Stanley Cup for ice hockey was established in 1893

A GOOD YEAR

B. Vulcanized rubber, which makes natural rubber stronger, more flexible and more resistant, and is used for modern tyres.

A SAVING PLAN

Daylight saving time

TYPESET

Johannes Gutenberg

WHAT WERE THEY?

They were all items of clothing.

1. A chiton was a tunic worn by the ancient Greeks
2. A liripipe was the long tail of a hood worn in medieval Europe
3. A banyan was a loose dressing gown, modelled after the Japanese kimono, worn in Western Europe in the seventeenth and eighteenth centuries
4. A polonaise was a two-layer

women's gown originally introduced in the late 1770s

5. A stola was a pleated dress worn by Roman women
6. Chopines were high platform shoes worn by women from the fifteenth to seventeenth centuries to protect dresses from mud and soil

A BUSY DECADE

B. 1770s

49ERS

Prospectors who rushed to California in 1849 following the discovery of gold there the previous year

A FRENCH SEQUENCE

The order in which they were sent to the guillotine in France after the French Revolution

CODE NAMES

They were the code names for the nuclear bombs dropped on Hiroshima and Nagasaki in Japan that ended the Second World War

WORLD LINK

They have all been titled 'the Great'

STATE OF THE UNION

Texas

WHO LIVED HERE?

General Robert E. Lee, the head of the Confederate forces. It was owned by his wife, Mary Anna Custis Lee.

RENAMED

The Kingdom of Saudi Arabia

NOTES